TV-Philosophy

TV-Philosophy

Series Editors:
Sandra Laugier, Martin Shuster, Robert Sinnerbrink

Television with Stanley Cavell in Mind
edited by David LaRocca and Sandra Laugier (2023)

TV-Philosophy: How TV Series Change our Thinking
Sandra Laugier (2023)

TV-Philosophy in Action: The Ethics and Politics of TV Series
Sandra Laugier (2023)

TV-Philosophy

How TV Series Change
our Thinking

SANDRA LAUGIER

translated by
DANIELA GINSBURG

UNIVERSITY
of
EXETER
PRESS

First published in 2023 by
University of Exeter Press
Reed Hall, Streatham Drive
Exeter EX4 4QR
UK

www.exeterpress.co.uk

Series title
TV-Philosophy

This book has received funding from the European Research Council (ERC)
under the European Union's Horizon 2020 research and innovation programme
(grant agreement N° 834759)

British Library Cataloguing in Publication Data
A catalogue record for this book is available
from the British Library.

https://doi.org/10.47788/ILDG2292

ISBN 978-1-80413-021-6 Hardback
ISBN 978-1-80413-022-3 ePub
ISBN 978-1-80413-023-0 PDF

Cover image © iStockphoto/WhataWin

Typeset in Adobe Caslon Pro by S4Carlisle Publishing Services, Chennai, India

We cannot see the moral interest of literature unless we recognize gestures, manners, habits, turns of speech, turns of thought, styles of face as morally expressive—of an individual or of a people. The intelligent description of such things is part of the intelligent, the sharp-eyed, description of life, of what matters, makes differences, in human lives.

Cora Diamond, *The Realistic Spirit: Wittgenstein, Philosophy, and the Mind*, reprint (Cambridge, MA: MIT Press, 1995 [1991]), 375.

The question what becomes of objects when they are filmed and screened—like the question what becomes of particular people, and specific locales, and subjects and motifs when they are filmed by individual makers of film—has only one source of data for its answer, namely the appearance and significance of just those objects and people that are in fact to be found in the succession of films, or passages of films, that matter to us.

Stanley Cavell, 'What Becomes of Things on Film?', *Philosophy and Literature* 2, no. 2 (1978), 256.

'You know the codes as well as I do. They're in every western, film noir, and melodrama we watched on TV as kids. What right do you have to ignore the moral you were taught, as was I, by popular entertainment?'

Paul Dédalus (Mathieu Amalric) in *My Golden Days*, Arnaud Desplechin (2015).

The sense we now have for essential characteristics of persons and objects is very largely the *result* of art.

John Dewey, *Art as Experience* (New York, NY: Perigee, 1980), 294.

Contents

Introduction

This book is one of two volumes that result from a decade-long enterprise in writing about TV series. The project developed out of a monthly column for the French newspaper *Libération* (2013–2022), which led to a book *Nos vies en séries* (2019) and an ongoing European Research Council project 'Demoseries', which explores a corpus of 'security TV series' from conception to reception.

These two new books provide English-speaking readers with access to my work on TV series for the first time. *TV-Philosophy: How TV Series Change our Thinking* is a theoretical monograph discussing the philosophical thought of series—the thought about the world that is produced and expressed through TV series—a Series-Philosophy akin to the Film-Philosophy developed by Stanley Cavell, William Rothman, Robert Sinnerbrink, and others.

The companion volume, *TV-Philosophy in Action: The Ethics and Politics of TV Series*, can be seen as that Series-Philosophy put into practice. It offers readers a selection of my columns from *Libération*, brought together with other writings from the online journal *AOC* (https://aoc.media/), *Le Monde*, and *l'Obs*. These pieces focus on individual series, or groups of related series, and films. Together, they may be taken as exemplars of a body of Series-Philosophy. The *Libération* columns in particular were often written in close proximity to the viewing experience, and are informal in tone: I write as a philosopher of ordinary language and a fan of series.

These two books—the more theoretical overview provided by *TV-Philosophy: How TV Series Change our Thinking* and the more specific and particularized *TV-Philosophy in Action: The Ethics and Politics of TV Series*—are envisaged as complementary. They can be read one after the other or in tandem; that is to say, dipping in and out of *TV-Philosophy in Action* for exemplars, while digesting the theoretical arguments of *TV-Philosophy*. An index of series, with references to all pages on which each series is mentioned, is included at the end of each book.

***

I am not an expert on television series, the media, or popular culture. This book and its companion volume do not claim any scholarly erudition or historical or aesthetic expertise. Rather, both books are the contribution of a philosopher of ordinary language and a passionate amateur—in other words, a fan—of series, to the collective reflection that is produced daily by not only critics, sociologists, and theoreticians, but also the mass of viewers and fans who comment on, evaluate, and discuss TV series. I am not interested in viewing series through some philosophical lens—quite simply because philosophy is not a lens, but rather, as the work of Ludwig Wittgenstein has taught me, an activity that leads us to examine our discourses and lives. Nor am I interested in producing a 'philosophy of series' that would take television series as its 'object'— for the simple reason that philosophy itself is completely transformed by our interest in these forms of popular culture, just as it was by cinema, which, as Stanley Cavell has shown, found its place in our world through its particular affinity with our ordinary experience. Our experience is profoundly affected by these works; as John Dewey wrote, it results from them: 'Instead of fleeing from experience to a metaphysical realm, the material of experiences is so rendered that it becomes the pregnant matter of a new experience. Moreover, the sense we now have for essential characteristics of persons and objects is very largely the *result* of art.'[1] In addition, the philosophy I try to practise is inspired by the ordinary language philosophy of Wittgenstein, J.L. Austin, and Cavell,[2] and thus consists in avoiding any position of superiority over ordinary culture.

Today, nearly everyone likes or is familiar with at least a few TV series. But the format is still simultaneously, and inextricably, under- and over-valued. There is a striking discrepancy between, on the one hand, series' intellectual, political, and moral influence, the place they occupy in everyday conversation and life, the often indulgent adulation they inspire, and, on the other hand, the lack of real interest in or even acknowledgement of them as works of thought. It is as if, in appreciating series, viewers and critics primarily valorize themselves, rather than trying to recognize or explain the influence series have over them. My aim here and in *TV-Philosophy in Action* is to elucidate or clarify series' particular power, and their thought—not in the sense of that which is thought about them, but rather the thought that they produce about the world in which we live. This is something that has gradually come to be recognized in cinema, which is now analysed as 'thought' in its own right, and not merely as an object of thought.[3] Thus, I am interested in pursuing a philosophy of series, but in the sense of the philosophy that series offer and produce—and for which they do not need the assistance of philosophy as discipline.

Philosophy has a penchant for discussing 'objects' that are outside it (this could even be said to be its stock in trade: 'the philosophy of X'), including the objects of popular culture, and this proclivity reveals its natural tendency to attribute a sovereign role to itself. But rather than providing philosophy with material for reflection or a reservoir of examples, the objects of popular culture constitute experiences, visions of the world that can stand on their own—just as philosophy does. My approach is inspired by Cavell's works on film, which he wrote at a time when American comedies—the comedies of remarriage[4] (sometimes referred to as 'screwball comedies') he studied in *Pursuits of Happiness* and the melodramas (sometimes referred to as 'tearjerkers') to which he later dedicated *Contesting Tears*—were not taken entirely seriously.[5] When Cavell began studying these films within philosophy, he was met with some perplexity, since they were thought of as popular entertainment, commercial objects devoid of cultural legitimacy or relevance—and, of course, their gendered nature meant they were further denigrated. The genius of *Pursuits of Happiness* lies in its method, which consists in taking these comedies seriously—not as objects offered up to the intelligence of the philosopher, who can use them as examples to reveal hidden mechanisms that might have escaped the director's notice (but not the philosopher's), but rather in order to show the intelligence inherent in the material itself, the intelligence a film brings to its own making. Often, philosophy claims that the genius of a work of art—especially a work of popular art—is discovered through analysis. Cavell showed, first, that these Hollywood movies were great works of art (although that in itself was not his focus; and at least with TV series there was never any debate over this point—or, if there was, it quickly turned into establishing a hierarchy between 'quality' series and 'trash'); and, second, that they contained intrinsic philosophical content. This is the method I use, and it is distinct from the approach of philosophers who look at cinema or a particular film not because they are of interest in and of themselves, but rather on the premise that philosophy reveals what is interesting about them.

Series constitute a form of experience that leads to philosophy in a particular way. Philosophy exists in order to describe and to clarify, and therefore to elevate, to raise oneself. This is in keeping with the ancient philosophical tradition of perfectionism—the impetus towards an expression of a perfect, or at least better self—a tradition that runs through these pages. It consists in helping people realize what they already know and in giving them the ability to philosophize using their own resources. Socrates was the first to practise this ordinary philosophy. Thus, we may say that philosophy is a way of empowering ordinary subjects, giving them the means to understand, experience, and take ownership of the world, as well as to educate themselves. This is a crucial aspect for approaching popular cinema and, above all, television series: to empower each individual to shape their own taste, create their own experience, and acquire their own competence and expertise.

When it comes to the objects of popular culture, everyone—including children—has the authority to say what they like and don't like; there is a form of trust in one's own judgement that is constructed through these works, a phenomenon that is often ignored. You don't need a degree to go to the movies. And yet—precisely for this reason—the expertise of the movie or TV critic or specialist is jealously guarded. It is this expertise that I have tried to democratize over the past decade in my column in the French journal *Libération* and in several other outlets (*AOC*, *Le Monde*, *l'Obs*). My method consists not in using these objects to set myself apart on the basis of some superior understanding, but rather in taking them seriously and looking at how they teach each of us to see them. This method is democratic, in that it recognizes each person's competence. Studying series is thus one element of my work on the democratization of democracy, which I have pursued in collaboration with the sociologist Albert Ogien in a series of publications.[6] But this method is not the 'by-product' of a broader reflection on democracy, for television series are a form of life that—like cinema—has contributed in a major way to strengthening democratic claims, by allowing each individual to master, or at least to trust, their own cultural choices and perceptions, in the process transforming the very meaning of democracy. Consequently, the analyses in this book are often oriented toward a political reality (the election of Donald Trump in the United States played an important role in their inception), and the twenty-first century has proven to be a time of exceptional dynamism for political TV series, which have followed the ethical blueprint of *The West Wing*, as I show throughout the book. The discussions that follow also often incorporate popular movies that share the same ethical stakes as political TV series, belonging to the same family.

Although many people appreciate TV series, few find art in television. Cavell himself was reluctant and somewhat dismissive.[7] My goal here is to discuss TV series as works that are, as Martin Shuster points out in the introduction to his groundbreaking book *New Television*, 'comparable in their form and function to (great) novels or films'.[8] Thus, this book explores the ethical, political, and philosophical meaning of works that use the medium of the 'televised' series. As Shuster notes, the rise of Amazon and Netflix over the past years has shown that series no longer need to be tethered to the object we call 'television', but all series use the qualities specific to the televisual medium—including when they expand or subvert those qualities. In other words, series are produced and caused by the fact of television. In the twentieth century, Cavell wrote: 'Certainly I have been among those who have felt that television cannot have come of age, that the medium must have more in it than what has so far been shown.'[9] Today, we can say, with Shuster, that television's time has come, that it has reached full maturity in the twenty-first century, and that our task now is to trace the consequences of this.[10]

When Cavell's 'The Fact of Television' was published in *Daedalus* in 1982,[11] television was still very much a 'theme out of school', to quote the title of the volume in which it was later included. Since the early 1980s, however, much has changed. First, the field of television studies has entered the main-stream academy, with television becoming the subject of a number of philosophical investigations. Second, starting in the 1990s, television fiction has been profoundly transformed. Many important shows now constitute an actual corpus of TV. This new reality of television includes the new-found power of TV series and the hold they have over contemporary viewers. This power arises, at least in part, from television's ability to integrate into everyday life and from the constancy of our contact with its fictional characters, sometimes over years or decades.

Cavell defined the ontology of film in terms of 'the question what becomes of particular people ... of specific locales, and subjects and motifs when they are filmed'—and added that the 'source of data' for answering this question is 'just those objects and people that are in fact to be found in the succession of films, or passages of films, that matter to us'.[12] In this sense, Cavell may have appeared to be right in 'The Fact of Television' when he denied that there could ever be great works of television, based on the television of the time. Yet this book is meant to show that his prediction about our future form of life with series was wrong, because today, series have expanded exponentially beyond their origin in the traditional TV set, thanks in no small part to digital media, networks, and platforms.

'To say that masterpieces among movies reveal the medium of film is to say that this revelation is the business of individual works, and that these works have a status analogous to traditional works of art.'[13] It is not that Cavell believed that television had no aesthetic interest (and he actually watched a lot of it, in addition to movies). But he believed he could only investigate what that aesthetic interest is by pondering what television is. The question is ontological. Employing the terminology of *The World Viewed*,[14] he posed the question: what is the medium's material basis? The expressive possibilities of cinema as an aesthetic medium are created by their realization, their actualization within a body of work that gives them meaning. For Cavell, the potentialities of the medium—in particular its technical potentialities—are not even possibilities as such as long as they have not been given meaning within a particular work.

As William Rothman notes,[15] 'when Cavell wrote "The Fact of Television," soap operas were primarily relegated to daytime, as they had all been before *Peyton Place* (Paul Monash, NBC) which premiered in 1964', and there were few prime-time American series until *Dallas* and *Dynasty*. At the time, television's dominant fictional mode was what Cavell (quite dismissively) called a 'series' (sitcoms such as *I Love Lucy*, cop shows such as *Dragnet*). In a series, in Cavell's sense, every episode tells a complete story that begins when a baseline of normality, the realm of the everyday, the ordinary,[16] a crucial concept for Cavell, is disrupted by a crisis, and ends with the crisis resolved and a return to normality. In effect, the format is a formula for generating individual instances of a programme. By contrast, in a movie genre such as the comedy of remarriage, what we might think of as the formula— what *Pursuits of Happiness* calls the genre's myth—is reinterpreted and revised by each member of the genre. The formula does not generate the instances; the instances generate the formula. Between the 1980s, when Cavell wrote 'The Fact of Television' and 'The Advent of Videos', and 2000, television changed radically. Insofar as the experience of television no longer had to be tethered to what Cavell called 'monitoring' (in the sense that a surveillance camera monitors the uneventful or banal present, waiting for something to happen), the arguments in 'The Fact of Television' for denying that television programmes can be works of art were rendered moot—and not only because of the possibility of watching films at home. The untethering of television fiction from monitoring was a development whose possibility 'The Fact of

Television' in no way denies. The advent of digital video recorders and then later of streaming video, which made 'time shifting' an everyday practice, was as consequential for television as the advent of videos was for film.

Unlike film (which stretched back to the early years of the twentieth century), television had no prior history as a great art. Hence there was no repression, no failure of acknowledgement, to undo. What made video cassettes, DVDs, and streaming so consequential is that they allowed television as a medium of art to be born. A miniseries—the dominant format today—is not fundamentally different from a long movie, as Rothman says:

> Dickens novels were published in instalments, but those instalments have simply become chapters to us, and most novels have chapters. A miniseries has a narrative trajectory known to each episode's writers. In principle, there's no problem making the protagonist, and ideally other major characters as well, undergo the kind of metamorphosis screenwriters call a 'character arc'—the kind of metamorphosis, so traumatic as to be tantamount to death and rebirth, that the women in remarriage comedies undergo.[17]

In what Cavell calls a series, every episode resolves the crisis precipitated by an inciting incident and ends with a return to normality, the realm of the ordinary. Only characters whose role is limited to the episode in which they appear are candidates for a kind of perfectionist metamorphosis. In 'The Fact of Television', Cavell observes that *Hill Street Blues* 'seems to be questioning the feature of a series [in his sense] that demands a classical ending for each instance, hence questioning the distinction between soap opera and series'.[18] Soap operas were the other dominant TV form at the time, and *did* allow for character progression, but owing to their connection to domestic subject matters and gendered audiences, they couldn't be candidates for series as art, according to Cavell. *Hill Street Blues* indeed pioneered this hybrid format when it premiered in 1978. It interwove stories about the professional lives of police officers with ongoing stories revolving around their personal lives, and thus was the ancestor of *NYPD Blue*, one of the first major TV shows of the 1990s to begin to transform TV formats, along with *ER* and *LA Law*. The 'procedural' side of such series was essential to shaping the format; it harkens back to the movies Cavell cites in *The World Viewed*. Cavell understood that there was a turn toward the depiction of professional lives concurrent with the turn toward scheduling TV fiction in 'prime time'. In 1982, Cavell could not know that these 'hybrid' series would soon dominate, and would revolutionize television fiction. He also could not know that the domination of this hybrid format would be limited to a few decades.

So Cavell was wrong about television, and of course he was also right. *Pursuits of Happiness* was a transitional work within Cavell's oeuvre, and shifted focus from the material basis of film to the conditions of a particular medium and to a series of works that earn their place within the tradition of moral perfectionism. In 'The Fact of Television', Cavell could not write about television the way he wrote about film in *Pursuits of Happiness*, given the essay's contention that, unlike a genre such as the comedy of remarriage, a television format is not an artistic medium. Popular culture is defined precisely by the creativity specific to genre, which drives the creation of works. For example, given how seductive the character played by James Stewart is to the heroine of *The Philadelphia Story* (George Cukor, 1942), the movie could easily have ended with their marriage—a possibility the movie briefly alludes to. But, as Cavell notes, it is the genre that decides—just as we know, without needing any confirmation, that *War of the Worlds* (Steven Spielberg, 2005) will also end with a remarriage (as most catastrophe movies do) and just as genre allows us to understand the somewhat embarrassing ending of *The Affair*, which depicts the reconciliation of the original couple as seen from an apocalyptic future. Thus, cinema is full of explicit references to archetypal works and to the genres that these works contribute to, in a given period. TV series are themselves a compendium of such references: references to films or classical series through the 'citation' of scenes or actors. It is the openness of genre and its creativity that make possible its later productivity, including in the derivation of new genres. TV series have clearly inherited the conversational capacities of couples from the comedy of remarriage genre, which has given them the grammar of their expressions, interactions, and emotions. Early twenty-first-century series have supplied forms of morality to an entire range of current genres: Mafia/cartel shows such as *Narcos* draw from *The Sopranos*; political shows such as *Baron Noir* draw from *The West Wing*; metaphysical shows such as *The Leftovers* draw from *Lost*; and feminist ones such as *Girls* or *I May Destroy You* draw (remotely) on *Sex and the City*. Thus, genre contains an element of empowerment for the generations of characters that follow, and it provides an expressive grammar, including for the viewer, who finds within it resources for their own feelings and situations. This creative aspect of genre, already present in cinema, has become more radical with TV series, which are explicitly terrains of ordinary expression and are themselves filled with moments of conversation about the recent or classical works that constitute their referential and moral universe, and with constant allusions to other TV and movie characters. Thus, the viewer's ordinary competence is a capacity for expression furnished by their knowledge, or mastery, of a genre. Genre is not essence: its value comes from the expressive possibilities it opens for both actor and viewer. Genre provides proof of concept of popular culture, of the fact that an experience is literally shared between creators and viewers.

In order to grasp the importance and interest of popular culture, an ordinary approach to philosophy and a particular understanding of morality are needed. Morality has traditionally been understood as a set of general rules, principles to be put into action. Popular culture completely shifts the traditional bounds of morality, by showing that literary, cinematic, and televisual works have strong ethical dimensions and function as forms of moral public education.[19]

This is what constitutes the ordinary virtues of these works: morality is to be found not in examples or general rules, but rather in characters from novels, movies, or series as they face ordinary life situations that present specific ethical problems. The moral dimension developed by popular culture is far from an ethics of duty, from grand universal principles that would apply to everyone in the same way. And ethics is not necessarily contained in judgement and action alone; it can also be found in a character's way of being, or how they are presented. The attachments we form over time to the evolving characters of series or even movies have to do with such characteristics, which are not usually seen as part of morality. Thus, there can be a form of moral education provided by figures who are not exemplary. In addition, movies and series are accessible to all: they can awaken the competence and appetite for life of all, and each of us has (and feels that we have) legitimacy to speak about them. This legitimacy is multiplied by social media, but ethically and politically it is rooted in the aspect of film and television that corresponds to our contemporary expectations with regard to democracy: democracy can only survive if everyone has a voice within it, and it requires a perspective in which everyone seeks to go beyond themselves, to become what they imagine as a perfect or better version of themselves. Although other forms of popular culture can lend themselves to similar analysis, the objects I discuss here and in TV-Philosophy in Action—popular films and TV series—teach and constantly express the idea that we must trust in the human desire to perfect oneself, to move toward the best. My goal has always been to support this desire at the philosophical level, and if others are tempted to label this populism, that is because they do not sufficiently trust people: for some strange reason, they think that when it comes to aesthetics and politics, ordinary people are not in the best position to make decisions about that which affects them.

The existing interest in popular culture and the obvious enthusiasm for television series have not yet led to a collective capacity to consider them as philosophy research subjects in their own right. What gives series their power and makes them innovative is the way they are integrated into our daily lives. It is our ordinary and repeated contact with characters to whom we become close, not in the classical model of recognition and identification, but rather of contact and affection. It is series' ability to educate us and to make us grow through our attachments to characters over the long course of their lives, and to groups whose interactions include and animate us. Characters constitute series' primary ontological contribution, and it is they who create viewers' attachments to these works. They are particular entities in which the narrative, the actor, and our own lives—as well as other elements—intersect. They are the basis for the ongoing conversation that viewers have with their own moral conceptions in watching.

The question of the relevance and importance of series is not just a question of aesthetics, sociology, or communication. It is, in addition, the question of how the presence of a practice within our societies (a wide-ranging presence, because there are now series in all countries, and today they circulate far beyond their countries of origin) changes not only our visions of the world, but also the world itself. Television series—and the place that they and their worlds have come to occupy in viewers' lives—are a phenomenon that everyone can observe within everyday life—if not within their own life, at least in that of others. Recently, this phenomenon has been profoundly transformed by digital media platforms (Netflix first and foremost now joined by many others), which have to a certain extent rendered shows independent from the traditional television set and the temporality that formerly inscribed them within larger social rhythms—the return of the television season; the weekly episode. And yet at the same time, such rites and rhythms have returned to the fore with widely viewed major series such as *Game of Thrones*, which fans continue to watch in the traditional manner while also engaging with them on the Internet through tweets, memes, clips, and so on.

My central point in the following analyses is that television series teach us about paying attention to forms of life. A bit like parents, families, and societies, they initiate us into what Wittgenstein defines as *Lebensformen*, vital forms or configurations of human coexistence whose texture is the result of the practices and actions that produce or modify them. They are also ideal sites for perceiving ways of being: of people, relationships, and family resemblances. A character's moral vision is publicly revealed or intimately developed through their use of language—their choice of words, their style of conversation. Television series thus pursue the quest for the ordinary and the pedagogical task defined by Cavell and taken up by popular cinema: that of providing a subjective education through shared experience and expression. Here I am again invoking the tradition of ordinary language philosophy that I have inherited from Wittgenstein and Austin, who defined language as voice, conversation, and practice. The invention of sound films constituted a historical step in giving voice to humans and, within certain genres, to women in particular. TV series are a further technical development that has continued this progression in a more diverse way and by giving a place and voice to a wider variety of people.

For Cavell, the importance of cinema is defined by its place in our ordinary lives. For me, a cultural form's contribution to moral perception is part of its value, and means that reception is much more than passive reception; it is, rather, a form of sensitivity, of mobilization, and of improvisation. Two facts interested Cavell in the value of popular cinema: first, the indisputable fact—which sets movies apart from other contemporary art forms—that cinema has had and continues to have importance for a large and socially and culturally heterogeneous audience: this is even truer of TV series. The second is the ability of each viewer to make their own choices within the multiform jungle of popular culture—of which TV series are certainly emblematic. Cavell also describes our experience of films as one of companionship, noting that we experience films in the company of chosen friends, in contrast both to the solitary experience of reading and to the experience of concerts or festivals, where we are part of a large collective. This notion of companionship can be applied to TV series as well: although, like movies, they can be appreciated solo, they are nevertheless objects of conversation that cross the boundaries of social class and sometimes of generations, including in anonymous exchanges on the Internet. This is the reason why many of my columns for *Libération* and other outlets (*AOC*, *L'Obs*, *Le Monde*) collected in *TV Philosophy in Action* look at how series (and some popular movies) can provide unexpected lenses through which to understand current events, as well as educational tools and instruments of thought and political struggle.

Nothing could be more foreign to my work than a view of mass culture as the alienation, manipulation, or intoxication of spectators (by this I mean that such a view is simply external to my work, rather than something about which I formulate a critique). Such a position clothes contempt for the public in the garb of criticism, and it is fundamentally anti-democratic since it presupposes that the critic is immune to such alienation. The strength of an approach that takes popular culture seriously is that it considers the public to be intelligent enough not to allow itself to be manipulated. For me, popular culture is not mass culture in the sense of a global, homogenous culture produced by capitalism that one may analyse for all sorts of reasons through social or economic critique. The democratic claim here is that everyone is capable of constructing their own relationship to the immensity of cultural production and of inventing themselves through the choices they make among its offerings. For anyone interested in series—not an easy interest to pursue, given the vast quantity of series available today on various channels and platforms—there are a certain number of anti-democratic stumbling blocks to be avoided. We must avoid seeing 'the public' or 'the audience' as a passive recipient, as if only critics and philosophers were granted the privilege of being able to distance themselves from the material. At the same time, we should be wary of elevating series into the philosophical sphere out of snobbery, in such a way that they become the prerogative of the theoretical jet-set, who alone are able to grasp their importance and to distinguish between what is sublime and what is junk. And, conversely, we must avoid the infantilism of pure fan discourse (here I cannot guarantee that I have always succeeded); the worshipping of 'great works' that are supposed to have given the TV format 'legitimacy'; the obsession with exhaustive knowledge of a genre, which in any case has become impossible at the individual level, but exists at the collective level on various websites. The fortunate trend of series being produced around the globe and viewed internationally furthers the democratization of the conversation.

***

TV-Philosophy: How TV Series Change our Thinking is the culmination of years of shared ideas and discussions with various family members, friends, and students. I would like to thank my children, Marie, Simon, and Ulysse, for introducing me to *Buffy the Vampire Slayer* and *Game of Thrones*, and for having shared *Star Wars* and other contemporary mythologies with me; I am grateful to Jocelyn for watching all the shows we loved with me, and some he didn't love so much. I owe so much to my late father, Jean-Louis Laugier, for the moments we spent watching *24* and *The Wire* together, a follow-up to all the American films he took me to watch at Idéal-Ciné, in Talence, in my youth. I owe thanks to all those on both sides of the Atlantic who have shared with me the project of acknowledging the philosophical importance of television series in the tradition of Cavell's work on cinema: Martin Shuster, Paola Marrati, Daniela Ginsburg, Sylvie Allouche, Thibaut de Saint-Maurice, Pauline Blistène, Hugo Clémot, Jeroen Gerrits, Hent De Vries, Mathias Girel, Philippe Corcuff, Perig Pitrou, David LaRocca, and William Rothman.

I am extremely grateful to my wonderful and smart editor, Anna Henderson, who supported this project, understood its ambition better than I did, and who, just like a super-capable producer, guided the two volumes of *TV-Philosophy* from its first concept through the episodes, and to the final product.

I would like to thank the wonderful 'Idées' team at *Libération*, especially Cécile Daumas, for their continuous stimulation and help with my monthly 'Philosophiques' column (2013–2022) on philosophy and TV series. These columns, and other short essays, are collected in *TV-Philosophy in Action*, which can be seen as the companion volume to this one and places individual series centre-stage. Writing for *Libération* has been an incredible piece of luck and a constant source of inspiration and liberation.

I am forever grateful to my friend Maxime Catroux at Editions Climats (Flammarion) who generously welcomed my first book on television, *Nos vies en séries*.

Many thanks to Daniela Ginsburg for her wonderful and insightful translation and to Tatsiana Zhurauliova for her astute reading. Thanks also to an anonymous, generous, and perceptive reviewer for some very helpful remarks.

And finally, I would like to thank the Master's students in my course on the philosophy and ethics of series at Panthéon Sorbonne (2015–2022). This book aims to show the crucial importance of integrating the material of series into any education worthy of the name—that is, any form of education that takes seriously the capacity of each individual to better themselves: one reason, among others, why *TV-Philosophy* owes more to Stanley Cavell than to anyone else.

Notes

1   John Dewey, *Art as Experience* (New York: Perigee, 1980), p. 294.

2   Sandra Laugier, *Why We Need Ordinary Language Philosophy* (Chicago: University of Chicago Press, 2013)

3   Stanley Cavell, 'The Thought of Movies', in *Themes out of School: Effects and Causes* (Chicago: University of Chicago Press, 1988), 3–26; D. N. Rodowick, *Philosophy's Artful Conversation* (Cambridge, MA: Harvard University Press, 2015); Martin Shuster, *New Television: The Aesthetics and Politics of a Genre*, illustrated edition

(Chicago: University of Chicago Press, 2017) are my main inspirations; and among other wonderful writings, Ted Nannicelli, *Appreciating the Art of Television. A Philosophical Perspective* (London: Routledge, 2017), Jason Mittell, 'The Qualities of Complexity: Vast versus Dense Seriality in Contemporary Television', in *Television Aesthetics and Style*, edited by Jason Jacobs and Steven Peacock, pp. 45–56 (New York: Bloomsbury Academic, 2013), Lorenz Engell, *Thinking Through Television* (Amsterdam: Amsterdam University Press, 2019) and *The Switch Image: Television Philosophy* (New York: Bloomsbury Academic, 2021).

4   The comedy of remarriage is a genre of Hollywood comedy films of the 1930s and 1940s that emphasized reuniting a central couple after divorce or separation. Stanley Cavell, in his classic book *Pursuits of Happiness: The Hollywood Comedy of Remarriage* (Cambridge, MA: Harvard University Press, 1981), coined the name for this genre. He argues that a group of seven films—such as *The Philadelphia Story, Bringing up Baby, The Awful Truth*—represent Hollywood's greatest achievement, in their philosophical depth and moral ambition, and through the presence of strong, independent, and sophisticated female protagonists.

5   Stanley Cavell, *Pursuits of Happiness; Contesting Tears: The Hollywood Melodrama of the Unknown Woman* (Chicago: University of Chicago Press, 1996).

6   Albert Ogien and Sandra Laugier, *Pourquoi désobéir en démocratie?* (Paris: La Découverte, 2010); Albert Ogien and Sandra Laugier, *Le principe démocratie* (Paris: La Découverte, 2014).

7   Cavell, 'The Fact of Television', *Daedalus* 11 (1982), and in *Themes Out of School* (San Francisco: North Point Press, 1984).

8   Shuster, *New Television*, 2.

9   Cavell, 'The Fact of Television', p. 76. See William Rothman, 'Justifying *Justified*', in *Series with Stanley Cavell in Mind*, edited by David LaRocca and Sandra Laugier (Exeter: University of Exeter Press, 2023).

10   Shuster, *New Television*, 2.

11   Stanley Cavell, 'The Fact of Television', *Daedalus* 111, no. 4 (1982): 75–96.

12   Stanley Cavell, 'What Becomes of Things on Film?', *Philosophy and Literature* 2, no. 2 (1978): 256.

13   Cavell, 'The Fact of Television', 77.

14   See Cavell, *The World Viewed*; Thibaut de Saint Maurice, *Philosophie en séries* (Paris: Ellipses, 2015).

15   William Rothman, 'Justifying *Justified*'.

16   Roger Silverstone, *Television and Everyday Life* (London and New York: Routledge, 1994).

17   William Rothman, 'Justifying *Justified*'. See also William Rothman's Foreword to TV-Philosophy in Action.

18   Cavell, 'The Fact of Television', 81.

19   Sandra Laugier (ed.), *Ethique, littérature, vie humaine* (Paris: Presses universitaires de France, 2006).

1

An Education

If the twentieth century was the century of cinema, the twenty-first century is undeniably that of television series. I am not one of those people who deplores the alleged end of cinema, although such dire predictions are increasingly common. Cinema is alive and well in our century, all around the world—although it is true that its most popular products tend towards serialization, as evidenced by superhero franchises with their mythologies of recurring characters.

As for television series, they were born last century of course. They had their first golden age in the 1990s, which included, in particular, the first two seasons of *Twin Peaks*, the various series created by the late Steven Bochco (*LA Law*, *NYPD Blue*, *Murder One*), and, of course, *ER*. But since the turn of the century (which marks an aesthetic turning point, just as there was a turning point in philosophy at the beginning of the twentieth century), television series have established themselves as part of our ordinary lives, becoming the subject of conversations and relationships, giving shape to our lives, and allowing us to discover more about the societies we live in. The importance of the phenomenon of television series, which gradually emerges throughout the newspaper columns that make up the companion book to this volume, *TV Philosophy in Action*,[1] is systematically underestimated, even as TV series enjoy increasingly massive success and are appreciated by larger and more diverse audiences. In addition, they are becoming increasingly more ambitious, as demonstrated by recent important shows such as *The Leftovers*, *The Bureau/Le Bureau des légendes*, and *Twin Peaks: The Return*, among others.

TV series are now in a moment of transition. Having matured, they are taken seriously and loved by audiences and critics, yet they are still not really seen as works of art or as subjects of scholarly research. It is as if their extraordinary importance in people's lives was somehow an obstacle to recognizing their true importance. Thus, my priority in this book is to highlight the realism of TV series, by which I mean not just that they are based on everyday reality, but also that they are now part of that very human reality. André Bazin taught us that what was revolutionary about cinema was that it took reality itself as its subject.[2] Similarly, television series take as their subject human reality and expression, embodied in characters we regularly spend time with—sometimes over the course of nine years, such as the neurotic heroes of *Seinfeld* or the group of *Friends*; sometimes over three decades, if we count all three seasons of *Twin Peaks* and thus accept the idea that its characters stayed with us during the twenty-six years that Dale Cooper spent in the Red Room. My thesis here and in *TV-Philosophy in Action*—the radical seriphilia that I defend—is that series, like other technical inventions of the past and of the present (mobile telephones and the Internet, which have developed alongside series, and vice versa), are constitutive of human life forms. It is in this light that they must be taken seriously, as resources for our education, both scientific and moral, and as giving us access to reality in new and previously unimaginable ways. From this point of view, it is outdated and unnecessary to see television series either as tools of mass manipulation that impose dominant visions of reality or as 'mirrors' of society that reveal its contradictions and problems. Instead, the importance of television series and their strength lies primarily in their capacity to provide an education in morality and to help us take ownership of our reality. They share this capacity with other forms of contemporary popular culture, which they voraciously integrate: comics, music, video games, detective novels, and so on. They are tools of democratization, not only in the sense that they are widely available, but also in the sense that they have the capacity to develop the political capacities of each and every one of us.

I am of a generation that grew up with movies and TV shows, together and inseparably. These were American, as well as French and British series from the 1970s—*The Persuaders!*; *Starsky and Hutch*—and from the 1980s—*Dallas*; *Magnum, P.I.*; *Miami Vice* (with Michael Mann as executive producer, already making a name for himself) and *Quantum Leap*. And, of course, I was already a fan: of *Columbo*, with Peter Falk); of *Moonlighting* (with Cybill Shepherd, and Bruce Willis's debut); of *Hill Street Blues* (the precursor of *NYPD Blue*). The characters on these shows, who were sometimes closer to caricatures than to characters, were part of me, just like the characters of the great films I discovered during those exceptionally formative years.

It is just as possible, and contestable, to speak of waves of series in the way we speak of waves of feminism. The 1980s represented the first wave, uneven but foundational. The 1990s brought the second wave, and the great classics: *ER*, *NYPD Blue*; and *Friends*, all of which shaped perceptions, influenced future creations, and inaugurated series as a form of life. The latter can be found in the ritual of waiting for new episodes each week; the rhythm of the long, impatient wait for the return of a television season; the establishment of the major genres (medical-sentimental, police procedural, shows about a group of young people); the existence of characters over the long term (an example being the character of John Carter, played by Noah Wyle, on *ER*, present throughout all the show's fifteen seasons, or Andy Sipowicz (Dennis Frantz) on *NYPD Blue*, not to mention the entire core cast of *Friends*), alongside newcomers whose departures become as painful as those of regular cast members. Among these numerous productions, one show stood above all the rest, seemingly coming out of nowhere: *Buffy the Vampire Slayer*, an incredibly innovative series that became a beacon of feminism through the figure of its super-heroine vampire killer, an exemplar of humanity and friendship.

Then, at the turn of the century, with the cable revolution, came the third wave. The great television series from this time are extraordinary works, and many of us were fascinated and transformed by them. David Lynch's *Twin Peaks* was no doubt the first of this wave of productions to be adored by fans and critics alike, followed by *The Wire*, *Six Feet Under*, *The Sopranos*, and *The Shield*. Just naming these series that radically revolutionized the medium gives an idea of the variety of subjects they dealt with, the breadth of their visual and narrative forms, and the aesthetic, moral, and political objectives they pursued. HBO's cult shows *Dream On*, *Oz*, *Sex and the City*, *The Sopranos*, and *Six Feet Under* dramatically raised the standards of quality for series, and not only because of the elitism of cable (which the viewer must pay for), but because of the ambitions and resources of these works, which aimed to be moral and aesthetic objects, in addition to pieces of media. This incredibly rich output from the turn of the century was followed by other masterpieces, both those produced by HBO in the wake of *The Wire* (perhaps the most beloved of all those cult series), such as *Six Feet Under* and *Deadwood*, and those from other networks seeking to follow in its footsteps: FX with *The Shield* and AMC with the legendary *Mad Men*, setting off a run of equally incredible productions from both networks that continued through *The Americans* and *The Walking Dead*, respectively. This wave clearly established new standards of quality for television writing. It was also the occasion for some to begin to claim, rather pretentiously, that TV series had now gained respectability (an irritating statement that is still heard today)—as if this inferior medium needed to prove that it could rise above its origins; as if 'quality' productions did not draw on earlier ones and were not based on the television medium as well as the perceptive 'know-how' of the television audience.

What we could call the fourth wave, that of the great series of the 2010s—*The Walking Dead*, *Game of Thrones*, as well as the lesser-known but equally remarkable US series *The Affair*, *American Crime*, and *This Is Us* and French series *Baron Noir* and *The Bureau*—developed in the context of a major change: the end of the era of the television set, and the rise of the giants of the digital realm as series creators. Some of the 2010s shows were still classic network shows. Yet Netflix no doubt became the HBO of the 2010s, with extraordinary series such as *Orange Is the New Black*, *Narcos*, *Stranger Things*, and a host of exciting series from countries across the world.

Just a few years ago, critics were gravely debating whether they should include Lynch's *Twin Peaks: The Return*—one of the most striking works of 2017—among the films of the year, and an absurd controversy arose over whether a film should be included at the Cannes Film Festival if it came out on Netflix. Alfonso Cuaron's film *Roma*, which was released directly to

Netflix the following year seems to have sparked less controversy on this count. Of course, a series is not a film. Over the past several years, I have been struck by just how much a good movie (of which there are still many) can convey, can evoke, and can show in just two hours (or a bit more); the immensity of the temporalities and landscapes it can traverse even now, when viewers are accustomed to longer formats (not only series with ten to twenty episodes per season, but also miniseries, which can be equated to long movies that last six or fifteen hours). I have never thought there had to be any rivalry between cinema and television; for me, it is rather a matter of succession and inheritance. I love seeing the Golden Globes bring movies and television together, celebrating an increasingly mixed community where the two modes of expression co-mingle, without any hang-ups. I loved seeing Adam Driver circulate from *Girls* to *Star Wars* (2015–2019), *BlacKkKlansman* (Spike Lee, 2018), and Martin Scorsese's *Silence* (2016) or Leos Carax's *Annette* (2021).

Of course, I am also fascinated by Benjamin Cavell's work and by his way of pursuing Stanley Cavell's writings on film in writing for TV. Cinema's end was already being proclaimed in the late 1950s, and the second half of the twentieth century was obsessed with this pronouncement. Both the declaration and the obsession lasted multiple decades and themselves gave rise to many masterpieces. Cavell's essential work *The World Viewed* was marked by nostalgia for an art form already defined by absence and the past.[3] During this same period, the first influential series that shaped my youth were coming out. It was Cavell's approach to the experience of cinema that allowed me to analyse TV series in the way I do here. Understanding movies not as works of art (which they undeniably are) but rather as shared, transformative experiences, whose important moments become moments in our lives, allowed me to demonstrate the particular value of TV series as constitutive of ordinary experience. Of course, this requires a kind of self-confidence on the part of the viewer, a validation of their own competence and capacity for reception. It also requires a conceptual revolution, which means liberating oneself, at least in part, from the criteria of cinematic good taste, and yielding to the seduction of what was long considered 'merely mainstream'. I remember that my high school peers did not know what to make of my love of *Saturday Night Fever* (John Badham, 1976) and the first *Star Wars* movies; my new college friends were equally perplexed by my enthusiasm for romantic comedies, the big Spielberg and John Carpenter movies (*ET*, *The Thing*, both from 1982), and movies such as *Back to the Future* (Robert Zemeckis, 1985) and the series of *Indiana Jones* (Steven Spielberg, 1981–). As we know, just like the Hollywood comedies of the 1930s–1940s, these works, which were beloved by audiences at the time, were overlooked by critics but are now considered classics alongside those by Scorsese, Leone, and De Palma. And they are still the primary grammar of my cinematic emotions. My real guides here were Serge Daney and Louis Skorecki, more so than major movie magazines such as *Cahiers du cinéma*—despite the richness and solidity of their choices, and their erudition, including in these popular domains. Skorecki was among the first to actually respect TV shows on the same level as films. I also grew up on the newspaper *Libération*, and the companion volume to this book is in large part made up of columns I wrote for *Libération* from 2013 to 2022 on TV series and on a few significant mainstream movies. Too often, 'philosophical' columns are dedicated to pontificating and to expressing certainty in the superiority of one's point of view, something I have tried to avoid.

For me, it is not a matter of 'philosophizing with series'; that is, taking examples from series to understand philosophical problems or concepts. No more than cinema, series are not a reservoir of examples or cases upon which to draw in service of reflections that pre-exist. Instead, the fact that many of us grew up with series in itself constitutes a philosophy, as if there were an affinity between the experience of series and experience in general. This is what Cavell observed with cinema: the proximity of the experience of the world and of film.

Today, TV series are so woven into the fabric of our lives that they cannot but shape our judgement and experience. What initially excited me about series and led me to write about them regularly (and I now realize that this regularity was itself part of my relationship to these works) was their way of producing, of being philosophy directly—independently of any usage of them as examples or illustrations, or of some critic showing how clever they are by 'discovering' the genius hidden in a mainstream product (and thereby, in the end, degrading the work they claim to be valorizing). The interpretation I propose here, which is inspired by Cavell, is based on two forms of trust: trust in the competence of the viewer and trust in the intelligence of the work as such. In the 1980s, within the academic world, Cavell had to fight to gain respect for popular Hollywood movies as forms of thought. At the time, cinema represented the idea of the popular—that which is accessible to all. TV series have now taken over from cinema the task of producing shared culture and transmitting values. As I have said, cinema is not over— quite to the contrary; it is becoming global—but the fragmentation of its audience and the disappearance of major movies that are not franchises (*Titanic*, James Cameron, 1997, and *Gladiator*, Ridley Scott, 2000, were the last movies with wide popular viewership to win Oscars) means that television has taken over the mission of educating a broad public, of expressing moral and political values. It does this through attachment to characters, to their styles and modes of being, to their specific tone in dialogue; thus, through the experience of the viewer, and the transformation of self that occurs as a result of regular contact with situations and characters. We are transformed by surprises and twists that cause us to entirely change our opinions about a character or plotline, and we ourselves change as we observe the physical changes characters undergo (e.g., young people who grow up, like the children on *Game of Thrones*, or older characters whose hairstyles or physiques evolve). This attachment to characters by way of our perceptions of the actors who play them is what leads us to take care of them, and, reciprocally, means that they take care of us—helping us to continue on well after a series has ended:[4]

'On film the actor is the subject of the camera, emphasizing that this actor could (have) become other characters (that is, emphasizing the potentiality in human existence, the self's journeying), as opposed to theater's emphasizing that this character could (will) accept other actors.'[5]

Walter Benjamin reflected on the consequences of new technical possibilities for reproducing visual and musical works of art.[6] Now, the widening of audiences for the arts, the development of popular cultures, and the establishment of new forms, actors, and models of artistic action and practice thanks to the digital turn are transforming the very definition of art and challenging elitist conceptions of 'great art'. In his 1936 essay 'Style and Medium in the Motions Pictures', Erwin Panofsky emphasized, as Irving Lavin notes, that 'film was first and foremost a medium of popular entertainment, devoid of aesthetic pretension, which reestablished the "dynamic contact between art production and art consumption" that is "sorely attenuated, if not entirely interrupted, in many other fields of artistic endeavor"'.[7] Today, this understanding and defence of an art that has not lost contact with its audience extends beyond cinema and into TV series: 'Rich and poor, those who care about no (other) art and those who live on the promise of art, those whose pride is education and those whose pride is power or practicality—all care about movies, await them, respond to them, remember them, talk about them, hate some of them, are grateful for some of them.'[8]

Another democratic characteristic of the experience of cinema is that in cinema we like the exceptional as much as we like the common. Television series are not movies, but they allow us to understand the aesthetic importance of the popular movies they are descended from, and, more generally, everything that has to do with the exploration of genres sometimes considered to be inferior because they are based on repetitive schemas or follow a formula: horror, romantic comedy, for example. In the case of cinema, Cavell writes that 'it is generally true that you do not really like the highest instances unless you also like typical ones. You don't even know what the highest are instances of unless you know the typical as well.'[9] This is clearly true of series, and viewers who are constantly on a quest for *the* quality series miss out on wonderful opportunities to shape their own aesthetic. Series are sites where subjectivity can be constituted, where tastes are both highly individualized and based on shared experience.

This goes against a certain approach to cinema that it is tempting to describe as French but which for Cavell represents the 'nightmare' of criticism: an obsession with aesthetics and with the movie auteur; an obsession with 'unique' works, to the detriment of recognition of the genres that define the history of cinema; an obsession with representation and image, to the detriment of the experience of a movie and its context—the people with whom one sees a movie, where one watches it, and the reason why. The aspect of companionship (the first chapter of *The World Viewed* is entitled 'An Autobiography of Companions') within the experience of cinema is at the centre of Cavell's analysis: 'It is the nature of these experiences to be lined with fragments of conversations and responses of friends I have gone to movies with.[10] We remember or experience a film differently depending on whom we see it with. This demonstrates to what extent the importance and significance of a movie are 'sensitive to context', as ordinary language philosophers would say.

In addition to personal experience, moviegoing entails a new definition of the private: 'we took our fantasies and companions and anonymity inside [the cinema] and left with them intact'.[11] This intimate companionship determines our viewing and our memory of the film: we bring those close to us to the movies, along with our private, inner world (this world is what defines the private, not the mythological private language that Wittgenstein criticized).

My reading of TV series and their various 'waves' is anchored in the understanding of cinema proposed by Cavell and in his goal of offering a change of perspective—which he called a revolution—on cinema and on popular culture in general (or American culture, which is often over- and undervalued in the same breath). It is hence necessary to take popular cinema seriously, to see its importance—to accept, as Cavell indicates in his essay 'The Thought of Movies', that Hollywood movies have as much to teach us about certain philosophical questions (such as the possibility of establishing contact with the world) as philosophy as we have known it until now does; and that there is, in the movies of Frank Capra, as radical a reflection on scepticism as there is in Hume or Kant. It is not easy to do this, and not only because of the lack of recognition of American culture, including and above all by itself. Too often, within cultural criticism, even genuine interest in popular culture is tinged with irony and pretension. One takes an interest in movies, TV series, or blockbusters with a false air of seriousness, and with the conviction that one is capable of finding interest in anything and of detecting the genius hidden in any and all material. Such supreme conde-scension, often on the part of philosophers, is bolstered by the embarrassing tendency of certain films to try to 'do philosophy'.

For Cavell, 'to take an interest in an object is to take an interest in one's experience of the object'.[12] To highlight the importance—whether aesthetic, political, or moral—of a television production is to describe one's own experience as well as the experience of others as fully as possible. Such an understanding of criticism is intimately linked to an understanding of, and commitment to, ordinary language philosophy. The idea that drives this book, as well as Shuster's important work, and which Cavell pursued throughout his career, is that there is a parallel between ordinary language (sensitivity to what we should say when) and aesthetic judgement (the discourse of criticism as the determination of importance).

To take series seriously, it is necessary to take popular movies seriously, to take oneself seriously, and to take Cavell seriously when, in *Pursuits of Happiness*, he compares the argument of *It Happened One Night* (Frank Capra, 1934) to that of *The Critique of Pure Reason*. Obviously, there is something shocking here—and that is precisely what interests Cavell. It is not the comparison between film and philosophy that is scandalous (for that has become quite common), but rather the fact of seeing them as equal in their projection of the world, in their competence and capacity for education. The philosophical relevance of a movie lies in what it itself says and shows, and not in what a critic might discover in it or develop on the basis of it. The 'nightmare of criticism' is to think that the only intelligence a film contains is the critic's, and not to see 'the intelligence that a film has already brought to bear in its making',[13] which includes the work of its actors. Audiences today, who go to the movies for the actors, are well aware of this, and Cavell's readings of movies, which focus on actors' embodiments of characters, and the types thereby created, and which we thereby learn to recognize (see Cavell's description of James Stewart's 'photogenesis' in 'What Becomes of Things on Film?') does justice to this ordinary tendency,[14] which is also a testament to realism (it is indeed the actors we see and it is their names that we use when we talk about a movie). The way in which, today, actors circulate from movies to series and back again (we may think of Nicole Kidman, Regina King, J.K. Simmons, Adam Driver, Glenn Close, Tahar Rahim Julia Roberts, and others), rather than movies being seen as a kind of promotion or step up from television (the usual example here being George Clooney's success) shows the interpenetration of the two cultures.

What Cavell calls photogenesis is actors' mysterious ability to render themselves perceptible to viewers, and in this way to constitute the viewer's experience. Just as movies fall into genres, and just as recognizing these genres is a form of competence, so the roles played by an actor fall into types—not pre-existing types, but rather types constituted, on the Wittgensteinian model of 'family resemblances', by the actor's performance. The cinematic type does not depend on the existence of a character distinct from, and transcendent to, the actor (as in theatre), but rather on the actor's appearance in various films: 'on film the type is not primarily the character but primarily the actor'.[15]

We can trace the emergence of a specific object constituted by the various movie roles played by an actor such as John Cusack, from his roles in movies for teens in the 1980s (*The Sure Thing*, Rob Reiner, 1985; *Say Anything*, Cameron Crowe, 1989), to those of his semi-mature phase (*High Fidelity*, Nick Hornby and Stephen Frears, 2000), to those he has played in maturity (which are a bit depressing, such as *Love and Mercy*, Bill Pohlad, 2014). Or we may think of the roles played by the immensely talented series actress Elisabeth Moss, from the girl she played in *The West Wing* to her role as a young woman on *Mad Men* and *The Handmaid's Tale*—not to mention on the series by Jane Campion, *Top of the Lake*, which over the course of its too-brief run demonstrated the interconnection between movie genres and series genres. Examining such objects would yield a new definition of cinematic and televisual works and objects, an ontology of the kind of interest we may have in characters and in the actors who carry these characters throughout their careers. It is particularly enjoyable, and above all, possible, credible, and surprising to see Kiefer Sutherland play the President on *Designated Survivor* because we have seen him, as Jack Bauer, save the lives of presidents. Seeing

Liam Neeson play Schindler in *Schindler's List* (Spielberg, 1994), Qi-Gon in *Star Wars*, and a martyr priest in Scorsese's *Silence* (2016) lends the actor a somewhat naïve moral consistency, which can be easily mobilized in the action movies he also enjoys performing in.

The audiences for cultural objects have changed since the end of the last century. The democratization of art in the digital age has not yet been sufficiently observed or analysed by philosophy, nor has the constitution of a new set of values through the wide distribution of certain series and the blurring of the distinction between amateur and professional in certain scenes, practices, and critiques. This has been because of a lack of study, adequate theoretical tools, and clear awareness of culture's shift toward the common. A profound transformation in the cultural field and its hierarchies is under way, and the change in attitude toward TV series within academic milieus is one of its marks.

Series have gone from being considered mind-numbing mass products to finally being seen as objects of study, as sites where artistic and hermeneutic authority is reappropriated, and where the viewer is re-empowered through the constitution of their unique experience. The critic Robert Warshow, one of Cavell's inspirations, wrote in his classic work *The Immediate Experience*: 'We are all 'self-made men' culturally, establishing ourselves in terms of the particular choices we make from among the confusing multitude of stimuli that present themselves to us.'[16] Today, it behoves us to map and examine, with new and diversified tools of cultural analysis, the democratization of art (in the sense both of its wide availability and its collective creation)—and, reciprocally, to study the emergence of artistic practices as resources for a renewal of democratic demands and forms.

The democratization of artistic production promised by Romanticism is realized in the new artistic forms and modes of participation and interaction that digital technology allows, opening the way for new forms of subjective authority. The question of democracy is thus also the question of our capacity for individual expression and unique aesthetic actions and choices. Art has gone from being a site of elitism to becoming an essential driver of social intervention and innovation, and of real democracy, if by democracy we understand not a form of government but a demand for equality and participation in public life. You no more need a degree to go to see a movie or, above all, to feel competent in judging it, than you need one, according to the ordinary language philosopher Austin, to speak ordinary language and to judge 'what we should say when'.[17]

The shift in interest toward 'ordinary' objects such as movies and TV series leads to a transformation of aesthetics. The theoretical stakes of references to popular culture are fundamental: it is not a matter of drawing from a reservoir of examples, but rather of reversing hierarchies of what counts. This allows for a new starting point for democratic thought and its perfectionist foundation, one based in Emersonian self-reliance and a Deweyian understanding of the public. In *The Public and Its Problems*, Dewey defined the public on the basis of a confrontation with a problematic situation: people experience a particular difficulty that they initially perceive as coming from private life, and a solution emerges out of the play of interactions between those who decide to give it public expression.[18] This makes it possible to redefine popular culture, and to see it no longer as entertainment without value, but rather as public moral education. In *The World Viewed*, Cavell took as his starting point film's 'popular' nature, connecting this to a certain relationship to ordinary life, an intimacy with the ordinary, the integration of film into the viewer's ordinary life; the way in which it is intertwined with everyday life and the constitution of the viewer's experience. An ordinary aesthetics must defend not the specificities of the individuals who created a work, but rather the shared and shareable aesthetic experience it creates/produces.

The arrival of a new 'democratic art' onto the scene inevitably leads to shifting conceptual boundaries: the meaning of the word 'work' is expanded, and those of 'artist' and 'author' are affected, as is the delimitation of genres. In losing their extraterritoriality, contemporary art and literature abandon their aristocratic aura and participate fully in the common space: contemporary art forms are discussed, reinvented, and reappropriated online, at festivals, and in workshops, displacing our conceptual categories, which were already challenged by the end of autotelism and of an aestheticizing conception of art. Does 'democratic art' belong to those aesthetics of the everyday that refuse to make art a sphere of activity separate from ordinary life? In that case, the emergence and establishment of 'democratic art' is not a new configuration within a larger, trans-historical system called art, but rather the most tangible manifestation of an aestheticization of existence, the realization of which entails the blurring of the distinction between art and the ordinary. Faced with the rule of algorithms, illusions of interactivity, and the frames imposed by the interfaces that invite storytelling, it is not a matter of contempt for 'the popular', but rather of seeing how cultural expressions and digital discussions serve, directly or indirectly, to enrich our relationship to the common, to the ordinary, and to ordinary political and ethical questions. We may see collaborative and digital practices of art as spaces of action where principles of equality, collaboration, and sharing are enacted and reinvented, both on the side of production and on the side of usage and interpretation. This leads to rethinking the relationship between art and democracy, and to doing away with rigid or institutionalized (politically and culturally) definitions of them in order to organize them pragmatically around actual, shared practices and forms of life.

The role of popular culture (not just TV series but also music, Internet videos, and so on) becomes crucial for reformulating ethics and for the political and social constitution of democracy. It is a matter of a democratic culture that is shared and that creates common values; a culture that is a resource for self-education, for the cultivation of the self through the practice of sharing and commenting on ordinary, public material that is integrated into ordinary life. What, in the 1970s, Cavell claimed regarding mainstream

Hollywood, whose films were underestimated at the time, now applies to television series, which have taken over from cinema, if not replaced it, in the task of providing a moral education to the public. Thus, popular culture can be seen both as a site where the young are trained and as a site for the 'education of grownups',[19] through the pooling and sharing of material that is readily available and can be shared in conversations.

Throughout his life, the question for Cavell remained that of the criticism that one can produce (and share) of this experience, and his philosophical ambition in *Must We Mean What We Say?* was to situate 'modernism' during a period when criticism itself was struggling with scepticism and had to recreate self-trust out of the ashes of experience. Cavell explains what led him to write about cinema at a moment when no other philosopher was interested in it:

> Film had for me become essential in my relation to the arts generally, as the experience of my extended bouts of moviegoing in New York and Los Angeles and Berkeley proved to me ... Philosophers, it seemed, had almost without exception left the field alone. Should this be taken for granted? Or oughtn't the fact of this neglect itself inspire suspicion? Given my restiveness with philosophy's treatment, or avoidance, or stylization, of human experience—a restiveness that is a treasured inheritance from my early reading of John Dewey and of William James—what better way to challenge the avoidance than through the worldwide phenomenon of cinema?[20]

Later, Cavell again evokes Dewey and James when he describes what he owes to their critique of empiricism: 'to take a fundamental, I hope imperishable, insight of Dewey and of William James—the way the classical empiricists distort or stylize experience'.[21] This dissatisfaction or agitation in the face of philosophy's avoidance (a key concept in Cavell) of experience— and in particular by philosophy that claims to be rooted in experience—is indeed what Cavell owes to his reading of Dewey, even if for him this reading was not sufficient to describe the unique experience of cinema—or, I would add, of television series.

One of Cavell's aims, and one of his greatest achievements, is to have shown the 'intelligence that a film has already brought to bear in its making',[22] which amounts to 'letting a work of art have a voice in what philosophy says about it'.[23] Understanding the relation of cinema to philosophy thus implies learning what it means to 'check one's experience', to use the expression from *Pursuits of Happiness*;[24] that is, what it means to examine one's own experience and to 'let the object or the work of your interest teach you how to consider it'.[25]

This means that one must educate one's experience so that one can be educated by it. There is an inevitable circularity at work here: having an experience requires trusting one's experience. This role of trust in education makes popular culture an essential resource for moral education.

Cavell raised the question of the moral component of 'public' works and the form of education they bring about in the public and private spheres created by contemporary forms of communication. The question of a morality expressed by contemporary forms of media is intertwined with all the dimensions of private and public life. This intertwining, which philosophers such as Hilary Putnam and Cora Diamond discuss in terms of morality,[26] is also an intertwining of modes of constituting a public. The address to the public becomes the constitution of a public discourse and of its norms, which are both sources of discourse and the product of this discourse from which they emerge. Thus, we are witnessing a shift towards a morality that is no longer normative or imperative, nor purely descriptive: an ethics of care in the sense of the particular perception of situations, moments, and themes offered to us in our intimate connection to the series that are part of our everyday life. Examining the moral discourse of TV series is important for constituting a pluralist and conflictual ethics. Neither a general principle, nor an abstract moral value, there is nothing spectacular about the care that comes from watching a series; it is one of those phenomena that are seen but not noticed, and which ensure the conservation and conversation of a human world.

Series depict both concern for others and the conflicts of care: perhaps most famously, *ER*, over the course of its fifteen seasons, repeatedly drew connections between the requirements of private life and those of work, and showed the conflicts internal to caring for patients (medically as well as morally), while raising a number of public health issues: AIDS, unequal access to medical care, abortion, disabilities, the end of life, and others.

French sociologist Sabine Chalvon-Demersay has analysed the type of moral education provided by the very form in which television series are presented, and the turn that took place in series beginning in the 1990s (with *ER* in particular), writing that it is the methodology and narration of TV series that give these works their moral value and accounts for their moral expressivity.[27] Key elements include the regularity of viewers' contact with series, the integration of characters into viewers' ordinary and familiar lives, viewers' initiation into new forms of life that are not explained—unfamiliar professional and social milieus such as hospitals, police forces, prisons, intelligence services, or the urban realities of cities such as Baltimore in *The Wire* and New York in *Sex and the City*, *Seinfeld*, and *The Deuce*—and the introduction of new, initially opaque vocabularies (without any heavy-handed guidance or explanation, as there had been in earlier productions). Recognizing this kind of moral education leads to revising the status of morality, and to seeing it not in rules, transcendental norms, or principles of decision-making, but rather in attention to ordinary behaviours and everyday micro-choices, to individuals' styles of expressing themselves and making claims. These are all transformations of morality that a good number of philosophers, weary of overly abstract meta-ethics and normative deontological ethics, have called for. Some, such as Martha Nussbaum, have tested morality on literary material.[28] But the material of TV series allows for a more developed contextualization and for a historicity of the public and private relation to it (e.g., through the consideration of regularity and duration). It allows for familiarization and an education in perception, in paying attention to the expressions and gestures of characters we come to know well and to the specificity of situations. Television series are indissolubly part of private life and the public domain: they are an interface.

As we have seen, Cavell broke with a critical tradition of seeing the intelligence of a movie as a by-product of its critical reading, and affirmed the importance of the intelligence that a film has already brought to bear in its making. This refers to the fact that the material itself educates viewers and critics alike, and that its relevance is not dependent on the critic's perspective. Cavell was the first to emphasize the importance of this point, and to call for the valorization, within criticism, of the role of screenwriters and producers as well as of the work of actors in creating the moral meaning and educational impact of a film.

Thus, the modes of expression (the moral texture, the style of speech and movement) of film and television actors are central elements of these works' moral contributions and of the reality they present to us. One task of criticism is then to demonstrate, in reading the moral expression constituted by series, the individual and collective moral choices, negotiations, conflicts, and agreements that form the basis of moral representation: the choices and trajectories of fictional characters, the storylines, and plot twists. The question of morality becomes a question of the interpretation of public choices and the development of a shared sensibility that is both presupposed and educated or transformed by these works. This is care for the public in all the senses of the expression, and an audience of care is constituted by this symbolic expression and the education it provides. Of course, there are good and bad kinds of education, but one that takes the moral capacities of the viewer seriously is indeed of the order of care.

These works are, in the tradition of Dewey, public, democratic forms of cultural production. The characters of television fiction are so well anchored, morally guided, and clear in their moral expressions—without being archetypal—that they can be 'let loose' and opened to the imagination and usage of each viewer; 'entrusted' to us, as if it were up to each one of us to take care of them. Whence the importance of the conclusion of series, which must teach the viewer to do without them, and, in this way, confide something to the viewer—a secret that is the series itself. The way in which certain series take care of the viewer, including through their endings, is one of the strongest elements of the medium's originality. Here we may cite the metaphysical ending of *Six Feet Under*, which, after recounting one death in each of its episodes, presents the death of each of the main characters in its finale, in order to reconcile us with our separation from them (and with our own finitude). We may also think of the ending of *Lost*, which concludes by teaching the viewer and the characters to leave the island forever while preserving the experience; or the last episodes of *Mad Men*, which gradually detach us from Don Draper by showing how everyone else learns to live without him. Or we may think of the conclusion of *Buffy*, whose heroine herself decides to bring the structural prophecy of the series ('in every generation there is a slayer...') to an end by sharing her power with all girls; or the conclusion of *The Americans* where the children of Elizabeth and Philip teach us to 'let go', to take leave of the series and its characters.

There is a moral, perfectionist quest in these series, in the hope they place in the capacity of the viewer to be educated. One of the innovations found in second-wave series is the way in which they confront the viewer with a mysterious world and vocabulary, the elements of which are not immediately understood, and thus oblige the viewer to pay attention, to gain familiarity, and gradually to educate themselves, like the child described by Wittgenstein at the beginning of *Philosophical Investigations*, who is integrated into an adult form of life.

Viewers are educated and cared for (attended to), as well as cared about (respected, taken care of) in their moral capacity. The writing of shows such as *The West Wing* and *Desperate Housewives* is based entirely on the desire for a collective, public expression of despair and on the hope for new conversations (the 'cities of words' in Cavell's title). It is a matter of creating a political site of expression for this despair and this hope, of the necessity of a caring democracy: the possibility of new forms of expression and of moral education, of something like public care through works that accompany people in their daily lives.

Martha Nussbaum has proposed defining ethical competence in terms of a fine-tuned and active perception (rather than the capacity to judge, argue, and choose).[29] For her, morality is a matter of perception and attention—not autonomy or argument. One objection to her approach is that it revives a caricatural opposition between sentiment and reason. But what matters here is recentring the ethical question around a form of ordinary psychology and around moral attention that is based on nuanced and educated perception. Moral competence is not a question of reason; it is a question of learning fitting expressions and developing sensitivity: for example, the education of the reader's sensitivity by a good writer, who makes a certain situation or characteristic perceptible to the reader by placing (describing) it within a suitable context. The education creates the meanings. This is why the model of description or vision (the orthodox or objectivizing model of perception) is not enough to account for moral vision, which consists in seeing not objects or situations but rather the possibilities and meanings that emerge within things, in anticipating and improvising at each moment of perception. Perception is thus active, not in the Kantian sense of being conceptualized, but rather because it is defined by improvisation and a constant changing of perspective.

TV series suggest, and require, a redefinition of ethics as a capacity for moral invention and attention to unique details. They teach us to see moral life as 'the scene of adventure and improvisation', which transforms the idea of moral agency.[30] This improvisation is at work in series, in our conversations, and in our perceptions, when we follow a dialogue with stupefaction, or when we find ourselves facing people or situations that have transformed us in ways for which nothing in our lives has prepared us.

Cavell uses the expression 'moral education', and speaks of 'pedagogy' in the subtitle of *Cities of Words*. For Cavell, whose childhood and youth were haunted by Hollywood movies, culture means popular cinema, whose productions were widely viewed at the time. The educational value of popular culture is not anecdotal. Indeed, to me, it seems to be essential to how both 'popular' and 'culture' (in the sense of *Bildung*) must be understood in the phrase 'popular culture'. Within such a perspective, the vocation of popular culture is the philosophical education of a public rather than the institution and valorization of a socially targeted corpus.

Thus, I have tried to do for series what Cavell did when he claimed the philosophical value of Hollywood movies and placed them alongside the greatest works of thought. Popular culture can be seen as the site of 'the education of grownups', who, through it, can attain a form of self-education, of self-cultivation—a subjective perfecting, or, more precisely, a form of subjectivation by means of sharing in and commenting on public and ordinary material that is integrated into ordinary life. It is in this sense that, as Warshow says, 'we are all self-made'.[31]

Notes

1   University of Exeter Press, 2023.

2   Bazin, André. *What is Cinema?* Vols 1 & 2 (Hugh Gray, trans., ed.). (Berkeley, CA: University of California Press, 1967–1971).

3   Stanley Cavell, *The World Viewed: Reflections on the Ontology of Film*, enlarged edition (Cambridge, MA; London, England: Viking Press, 1971). See also his *Pursuits of Happiness: The Hollywood Comedy of Remarriage* (Cambridge, MA: Harvard University Press, 1981); *Cities of Words: Pedagogical Letters on a Register of the Moral Life* (Cambridge, MA: Belknap Press of Harvard University Press, 2004).

4   See Cavell, *The World Viewed*; de Saint Maurice, *Philosophie en séries*; Sabine Chalvon-Demersay, 'Enquête sur l'étrange nature du héros de série télévisée', *Réseaux* 165, no. 1 (2011): 181–214.

5   Stanley Cavell, *A Pitch of Philosophy: Autobiographical Exercises* (Cambridge, MA: Harvard University Press, 1994), p. 137.

6   Walter Benjamin, 'The Work of Art in the Age of Mechanical Reproduction' (1935) (New York, Classic Books America, 2009).

7   Erwin Panofsky, *Three Essays on Style*, ed. Irving Lavin (Cambridge, MA: MIT Press, 1995), p. 11.

8   Cavell, *The World Viewed*, pp. 4–5.

9   Ibid., p. 6.

10   Ibid., p. 9.

11   Cavell, *The World Viewed*, p. 11.

12   Cavell, *Pursuits of Happiness*, p. 7.

13   Ibid., p. 10.

14   Cavell, 'What Becomes', p. 254.

15   Cavell, *The World Viewed*, p. 174.

16   Robert Warshow, *The Immediate Experience: Movies, Comics, Theatre & Other Aspects of Popular Culture*, enlarged edition (Cambridge, MA: Harvard University Press, 2001).

17   J.L. Austin, *Philosophical Papers* (Oxford: Clarendon Press, 1961), 182. See Laugier 2013.

18   John Dewey, *The Public and Its Problems* (New York: Henry Holt and Company, 1927).

19   Stanley Cavell, *The Claim of Reason: Wittgenstein, Skepticism, Morality, and Tragedy* (Oxford: Oxford University Press, 1979), p. 125.

20   Cavell, *Little Did I Know*, p. 423.

21   Ibid., p. 497.

22   Cavell, *Pursuits of Happiness*, p. 10.

23   Stanley Cavell, 'Something out of the Ordinary', *Proceedings and Addresses of the American Philosophical Association* 71, no. 2 (1997): 25.

24   Cavell, *Pursuits of Happiness*, p. 12.

25   Ibid., p. 10.

26   Laugier, *Éthique, littérature, vie humaine*.

27   Sabine Chalvon-Demersay, 'La confusion des conditions. Une enquête sur la série télévisée Urgences', *Réseaux* 17, no. 95 (1999): 235–83.

28   Martha Nussbaum, *Love's Knowledge: Essays on Philosophy and Literature* (New York: Oxford University Press, 1990).

29   Martha Nussbaum, '"Finely Aware and Richly Responsible": Moral Attention and the Moral Task of Literature', *The Journal of Philosophy* 82, no. 10 (1985): 516–29.

30   Cora Diamond, *The Realistic Spirit: Wittgenstein, Philosophy, and the Mind*, reprint (Cambridge, MA: MIT Press, 1995 [1991]), p. 316.

31   Warshow, *The Immediate Experience*.

2

Forms of Shared Experience

Note that the meaning of the expression 'popular culture' has recently changed,[1] so much so that we sometimes use it without really knowing what we are saying. Previously, 'popular' designated an undervalued domain (i.e., pop culture was not considered real culture), but over the past few years, it has begun to refer to a domain that claims its popularity as the very thing that gives it its value. 'Popular', in contrast to 'populist', has taken on a predominantly positive connotation. Who doesn't want to be popular?

As I mentioned earlier, Cavell defined philosophy in perfectionist terms, as 'the education of grownups'. This was in parallel with his goal of giving popular culture—for him, Hollywood movies in particular—the function of changing, even metamorphosizing, us. But what is this education? Cavell conceived of growth—once childhood and the phase of physical development are over—as the capacity to change. It is this capacity that is at work, for example, in the comedies of remarriage he studied, in which the lead couple mutually educate one another, and are transformed by their separation and reunion.[2] And it is this capacity that is at work in the moral perfectionism without which democracy is a dead letter. Philosophy, then, consists in bringing popular culture into one's imagination, one's language, and one's life.[3] This is the enterprise that Cavell named 'moral education'. For him, culture's value lies not in great art but in its ability to transform us.[4]

The way Cavell claims the philosophical value of Hollywood movies—placing them at the same level as the greatest works of art, yet without launching into empty reflections on cinema as great art—might be seen as populist, or even demagogical. My argument is that what Cavell attributed to Hollywood movies today has carried over into other modes of creation—not only TV series, but also video games, comics, and so on—which have taken over the task of educating adolescents and adults. These modes are the paradigm for what we call popular culture today, for that adjective no longer applies to art forms such as traditional songs or folklore, on which this culture was once based. Whether we like it or not, television series have become sites of the education of individuals, and thus provide a form of subjective perfecting that occurs through sharing and commenting on public and ordinary material that is integrated into everyday life. The reflections on TV series and movies that I present in this book consider the collective development of a popular ethics, through the works themselves and through the conversations they engender, both public and private.[5]

It is important to understand that for Cavell, the stakes of our relationship to popular culture are both ethical and political. His starting point was the popular nature of film, which for him conveyed a realism of the ordinary. This realism comes above all from the way in which film is embedded in our everyday life and integrated into our ordinary experience. This is what distinguishes it from the (other) arts: everyone cares about movies. Furthermore, we generally like exceptional movies as much as we do run-of-the-mill ones:

> The movie seems naturally to exist in a state in which its highest and its most ordinary instances attract the same audience (anyway until recently) . . . There are, of course, in literature a few instances of very great artists who are at the same time popular. But my claim is that in the case of films it is generally true that you do not really like the highest instances unless you also like typical ones.[6]

Cinema, in this sense, is not—or is not primarily—a matter of art. Rather, it can be thought of as an elementary form of shared experience. In fact, Cavell does not speak of 'seeing a movie', but rather of 'moviegoing': it is less a matter of aesthetics than of practice; a democratic practice that articulates and reconciles the private and the public, subjective expectations and the sharing of the common. The relationship of cinema to popular culture is largely shifted as a result. Cavell dismisses the idea that all art passes through a popular stage in its infancy, as if there were a hierarchy or natural evolution from popular art to great art. Panofsky's position was that cinema was able to take up the popular genres of tragedy, romance, crime, adventure, and comedy as soon as moviemakers understood that these genres 'could be transfigured . . . by the exploitation of the unique and specific possibilities of the new medium'.[7] Cinema as the exploration of new possibilities—this is a central theme in the philosophy of film. But it does not interest Cavell. Cinema is important to him because of the place it has in our lives. Moviegoing transforms our existence by educating our ordinary experience, not only in the classical sense of shaping aesthetic taste, but also in the sense of a moral training that is constitutive of our singularity. In fact, our particularity is never as obvious as in our choice of the films or series that mark moments of our lives. The ordinariness of popular culture emerges out of our capacity to define our uniqueness through our allegiances and values in relation to it; I am thinking here of things such as the 'Top 5' lists in the film *High Fidelity*, and more recently in the series *High Fidelity* (starring Zoë Kravitz), through which the characters not only enumerate but also literally are their tastes. Cinephilia is popular education of the self—not through some canon of universal masterpieces, but through the constitution of one's own list of favourite movies, scenes, and moments, which fit different circumstances and are remobilized for different occasions in life.

Thus, the ordinary realism of cinema is not primarily the result of its relationship to the real, although this ontological question has been widely discussed; its realism comes from its inclusion in real life. And it is the way in which each individual creates their own experience out of cinema that makes it a democratic art: the democracy of the singular. The adjective 'popular' in connection to cinema refers not only to its accessibility, but also to its basis in ordinary experience.

There is nothing easy about taking an interest in one's experience and knowing what matters for oneself. Cavell writes that 'without this trust in one's experience, expressed as a willingness to find words for it, without thus taking an interest in it, one is without authority in one's own experience'.[8] It is only in this way that a popular (and perfectionist) conception of democracy can be defined: through trust in oneself, which, for Ralph Waldo Emerson and Henry David Thoreau, is what justifies civil disobedience. Cavell contests the possibility of determining the importance of a film from a theoretical or historical point of view; democracy in general, and the democracy of cinema in particular, stands in opposition to condescension to or criticism of popular cultures. No reflection on the popular, including in political terms, can elide the issue Cavell takes on when he refuses both the critic's contempt for forms seen as degraded and the condescension of intellectuals who claim an interest in series or in B-series while being driven by the certainty that they are in a position of superiority with respect to the material or object they are analysing. As for Cavell, he bases his work on 'the intelligence that a film has already brought to bear in its making'.[9] The melodramas and comedies he discusses in his books demonstrate such intelligence. These films constitute a 'laboratory' for a moral conversation that can lead to 'the democratization of perfectionism'.[10]

Popular culture as common ground does the opposite of brutalizing the masses: it is today the site where non-conformist or non-capitalist values can be developed. The perspective opened by Cavell for popular movies is now applicable to TV series, as well as to anything that involves the exploration and mixing of 'genres' of culture. I have discussed the type of education provided by the very modality of series' presentation: the integration of characters into viewers' ordinary and familial lives and the initiation of the viewer into forms of life (cultures, professions, milieux, cities) that are not explicitly explained and are initially opaque. This method of series, their narra-tivity and form, gives them their moral relevance and democratic capacity. But this leads to revising the status of morality and, following Wittgenstein and Diamond, seeing it not in rules and principles established externally, but rather in attention to ordinary conduct, everyday micro-choices, and individuals' styles of expressing themselves and making claims. The material of TV series allows for contextualization and historicity (regularity, duration) as well as for familiarization and an education of perception (attention to the expressions and gestures of characters we come to know; attachment to them). In both mainstream movies and in series, this entity, the moral type—bound together by family resemblances and made up of the various roles an actor has played and their unique expressivity or way of being—rivals the mystique of the author and becomes an object in itself. The result is a new definition of a cinematic work or object as connected to the ordinary life of culture. Cavell notes that the writings of Warshow, a pioneer in the criticism of film and popular culture, required a specific attention and a personal form of writing, for such criticism refers to a radically new experience, one for which the inherited concepts we usually mobilize in our cultural adventures are of no use, and which have not yet been replaced by other ones: 'What he finds in these more everyday concerns he needs to write personally, but it seems clear that the reverse is equally true, that he wants to attend to them because that attention demands of him writing that is personal, and inspires him to it.'[11]

As I have noted, Dewey based his definition of a public on a confrontation with a problematic situation in which individuals experience a particular difficulty. Understood in light of this theory of the public, television inherits the task of moral education that Cavell ascribed to popular cinema. The characters of television fictions can be freed and opened to the imagination and usage of each viewer; they are entrusted to us, as if it were up to each of us to take care of and preserve them.

In cult series such as *Buffy*, *Game of Thrones*, and *The Walking Dead*, we find a moral quest that is perfectionist in nature and democratic in vocation—for these series aim for the ethical experience they provide to be shared widely. Such series depict one or more journeys of personal growth and testify to hope in the educability of the viewer, who is obliged to pay close attention. For Warshow and for Cavell, such perfectionism defines popular culture and its genres, which, as noted, constitute a family in the Wittgensteinian sense, rather than a specific domain that can be defined objectively by criticism. Thus, TV series become sites of education, an education that amounts to a form of subjective perfecting as individual viewers share and comment on public, popular material that is integrated into their lives. To focus on such ordinary aesthetics is to go against the traditional critical approach, with its obsession with 'great art' and the mystique of the auteur, with 'representation' and image, over and above the ordinary experience of viewing a film and the subjective—yet always shared and common—experience of public material.

For Cavell, cinema is one of the elementary forms of shared experience: it is less a matter of aesthetics than of practice, an ordinary practice that connects and reconciles the private and the public; subjective expectation and the sharing or creating of the common. Hence the importance of extending Cavell's aesthetic and ethical method to works that today are as widely viewed and popular as movies were in the twentieth century. Cinema is not dead; it is becoming even more creative and inclusive—but (for now) it does not have the same universal or even national impact it did in the twentieth century.

Movies, like TV series, present us with important moments in life, moments of transformation, which in our real lives are fleeting and indeterminate or require years if not an entire lifetime to comprehend. This is the self-education that cinema provides and by/through which, using Cavell's terms, we may define our own individual 'cinematic autobiography': the way in which our life is constituted of fragments of cinema, key moments around which we orient ourselves and are part of our lives in the same way that dreams or real moments that haunt us are. It is also an education in autonomy (or 'self-reliance' to use Emerson's concept): learning to trust one's experience and to make one's judgement independent.

Such content makes it possible to shift philosophical questions away from matters of judgement and moral choice and toward an examination of ordinary moral life, with its difficulties and impasses, in which each person has a voice. This requires taking seriously the moral intentions of producers and screenwriters, and the constraints thus imposed on televised works of fiction. Cavell, breaking with a critical tradition that made the meaning of a film a by-product of its critical reading, affirmed that the material itself educates both the viewer and the critic, and does not depend on the critical gaze for its relevance.

Cavell was the first to emphasize this point and to call for the valorization, within criticism, of the role not only of screenwriters and producers, but also of actors and the work they do in developing the moral sensibility and moral pedagogical impact of a film. Breaking with traditional criticism, which made the intelligence and meaning of films a by-product of critical interpretation, Cavell affirmed the importance of the collective writing of films, and of the function of screenwriters, directors, and also actors in creating films' meaning and educational value. The address to the public/audience also becomes the constitution of a public discourse and its norms. Morality is constituted by the claims of individuals, and by the recognition of others' claims; the recognition of a plurality of moral positions and voices within the same world. This answers the question raised by Cavell concerning the moral function of "public" works and the form of education they generate in the public *and* the private they create. This intertwining of the private and the public is also an intertwining of modes of constituting a public. These are public and democratic forms of cultural production; they are democratic in the sense that, as the proliferation of blogs, amateur criticism, and conversations about popular series demonstrates, they give each individual the capacity to elaborate and trust their own judgement. TV series and the place that they and their worlds occupy in viewers' lives clearly exist in relationship to individual experience.

This entanglement of the private and the public is an entanglement of modes by which a public or audience is constituted, and is also expressed in new modes of subjectivation. This brings us back, again, to the question of what matters for someone—without pointing to some falsely revolutionary, and ultimately condescending, inversion of 'real' aesthetic values. Series continue the pedagogical task undertaken by popular cinema, the task of providing an education that is inseparably subjective and public. It is a matter of a new evaluation of importance, something Wittgenstein called for when, in a magnificent passage in the *Philosophical Investigations*, he proclaimed the need for ordinary language philosophy and for attention to real life:

> Where does our investigation get its importance from, since it seems only to destroy everything interesting, that is, all that is great and important? (As it were all the buildings, leaving behind only bits of stone and rubble.) What we are destroying is nothing but houses of cards and we are clearing up the ground of language on which they stand.[12]

Cavell's point of departure in *The World Viewed* was Tolstoy's replacing the question of art's essence with that of its importance. Importance is not something extra, an afterthought, a supplement to essence. This is a grammatical procedure: the connection between the essence and the importance of a phenomenon is conceptual. Mastering a concept means knowing its importance: our criteria of usage spell out what counts for us, in the sense both of what is identified as falling under a concept (what 'counts as'), and in the sense of what matters, what arouses our interest and represents a value for us, emerges in our eyes.

To my mind, this centring of the important and of the personal within democratic thought characterizes popular culture and its genres, which constitute a family in the Wittgensteinian sense of family resemblances and are formed out of a contiguity in experience, rather than existing as specific domains that criticism and its criteria can render objective. Popular culture can only be defined as education in attending to ordinary objects and situations, in reacting to events and to others as they present themselves to us. Television is at the core of popular culture in the twenty-first century, as film was for Warshow and Cavell in the twentieth.

The injunction to take ownership of and recollect one's experience defines the new exigency of a culture of the ordinary, which is far removed from any laments about the alienation popular culture is said to cause—and, symmetrically, from any false enthusiasm for that which one thinks one can master and conceptualize without really taking it—and oneself—seriously ('taking oneself seriously' is one of Cavell's favourite expressions).[13] But it is also something that democracy requires of us: democracy, in terms both of aesthetic procedures and the invention of the public, is discovered in this 'personal' quest for words to describe an experience *that has precisely deprived you of the vocabulary you need to confront it*.[14] And this provides a possible definition of popular culture from the point of view of a politics of the ordinary,[15] which recognizes that each of us does what we can to voice our experience, and to make our voice heard. In that sense, TV series today represent a crucial link in the democratization of culture and of democracy itself, not only through their wide reach, but also though the work of self-reliance that accompanies them.

Despite the exponential increase in publications about TV series in the USA and in France, it seems that the research so far carried out has not entirely accounted for the role that series play in the education of the young and the public in general, in the transmission and sharing of values, in the development of democracy (both in everyday life and in institutions), in raising awareness of risks (e.g., terrorism or climate related), and in social inclusion and the integration of diversity in terms of gender, racial and ethnic minorities, and sexuality. Nonetheless, it is clear today, if we look just at US series, which have been distributed globally and are well known in Europe, that, for example, the show *ER*, in the 1990s, drew attention to a number of public health issues such as abortion, domestic violence, euthanasia, and disability. Similarly, the cult show *Buffy* played a significant role in promoting equality of the sexes among its adolescent audience. The series *24*, which launched in the immediate wake of the 9/11 attacks (although it had been shot well before), created an enduring awareness of the risk of terrorism and of the moral degeneracy of democracies engaged in a global fight against terrorism (i.e., their promotion of torture), while at the same time preparing viewers to see a black president on-screen. In Europe, shows such as the Danish *Borgen*, the wonderful French *Baron Noir* and *Hippocrate*, and the Spanish *La Casa de Papel* go beyond entertainment, striving to politically shape a sometimes cynical public and to re-enchant democratic life. And finally, post-apocalyptic series such as *The Walking Dead*, *The Leftovers*, and *The Handmaid's Tale* are an indication that greater attention is being paid to the risks of environmental catastrophes and a loss of ethical values. These works and these themes both reveal a moral state of the world and can be seen as tools of education, of moral perfecting, and of influence—also known as soft power. In the genre of security series—exemplified by *Homeland* and *The Bureau*—the entertainment industry's reactivity has been accompanied by an institutional and strategic reconfiguration that attests to the role of security fictions in contemporary conflicts: in the United States, France, and the United Kingdom, these series are increasingly developed in collaboration with actors from the world of defence and security (intelligence agencies), thus creating new ethical and political stakes and challenges.

Within this context, we can finally begin to reflect on the roles, effects, and forms of fictional and serial representations in popular culture and on how they might affect social inclusivity, the struggle against discrimination, the advances and awareness necessary for the security of persons and societies, the preservation of freedoms during crises, and, in general, the construction or consolidation of shared values. TV series are increasingly recognized as objects of research, but for the most part they have received attention within the fields of cultural studies (on the part of researchers specializing in the English-speaking world), aesthetics (as a sub-domain of film studies), and communications (where audiences and reception are studied). It would seem that the role TV series and popular movies can play in educating and consti-tuting 'a public', in transmitting and spreading values, in creating awareness of terrorist or climate-related risks, and in promoting social inclusion and diversity has not yet been recognized. And yet it is clear that US series from *ER* to *Game of Thrones* and *Homeland*, as well as an increasing number of popular, ambitious European series, have drawn attention to many social, political, racial, and security issues. Thanks to their format (the way that they unfold over time, their weekly and seasonal regularity, the fact that they are often viewed within the home), the attachment to characters they inspire, the democratization that the Internet has allowed (through things such as streaming, discussion forums, and amateur productions), they make possible an unprecedented form of education through the expression and transmission of public problems, particularly in terms of the diffusion of values, struggles against violence and discrimination, and 'human security' in general. It is now also possible to imagine new methods of education that will further advance cohesion and security, in particular through the transmission of knowledge to high school students and broader audiences via popular culture. Because of the wide audiences they reach, series can play a role in the preservation of the democratic spirit. They constitute a resource that can be mobilized to face the upheavals under way, drawing on a rich cultural and literary tradition, which, in Europe, has recently been marked by the development of remarkable French, Danish, British, and Italian series.

The social impact of TV series and of popular culture is thus a complex issue. Various thinkers within the philosophy of film have looked at the pedagogical and formational values of popular fiction and at a moral education that transmits forms of life rather than abstract norms. Their works focus on popular and classic movies, but only rarely has the moral and political impact of TV series been systematically studied. We must begin to envision series as linguistic, ethical, and cultural reference points that structure understandings of the world, produce knowledge, and prepare viewers to understand and confront threats. And we must take them as seriously as we do the great political films of the twentieth century.

Three major approaches have dominated 'standard' studies of TV series. First, since the 1990s, the sociology of media has occasionally turned its attention to topics such as how series are made, their reception and fan clubs,[16] and practices of consumption, in connection with the concept of popular culture.[17] The popularity of series has led to a proliferation of publications on the subject, in which the 'mirror' approach dominates: the idea that series reveal a certain state of the world, whether moral, political, or societal. But this kind of analysis does not allow us to understand that series can have an impact on audiences' moral values. A second approach, which may be called the aestheticizing approach, continues in the tradition of 'classical' film studies. In keeping with elitist film criticism, it prioritizes formal critical analysis, refuses any factual or psychological analysis, and only pays attention to 'ambitious' series—that is, those produced and shot by cinema auteurs (which is somewhat understandable, given that directors such as David Lynch and Jane Campion have made some of the best series).

And finally, the most fertile approach is the cultural studies approach, which seeks to examine cultural artefacts as part of a broader quest to understand societal phenomena within the context of English-speaking cultures.

What is missing is research that would bring together moral and political philosophy to examine the uses of popular culture (from films and series to games and sports) in consolidating or creating shared values. In France, the tradition of Kantian aesthetics, with its concept of 'disinterest', remains particularly strong in connection with film studies, which has meant that the field has remained disconnected from the reality of everyday commerce with images and their integration into daily life. Gender inequality has played a role in this refusal of or contempt for everyday life and for art forms that are too closely tied to it. The lack of legitimacy of 'minor' artistic genres is often expressed in gendered terms—melodramas or series 'for chicks', and so on. 'Orthodox' cinephilia focuses on the auteur, to the detriment of the viewer's agency. Thus, it looks unfavourably on the 'lay criticism' that occurs online, which is a remarkable resource for anyone interested in series—although I will not be focusing on these encyclopaedic aspects of popular culture here.

One interesting development for thinking about the uses of series is the multiplication of links between television professionals and those in the security domain in the United States, the United Kingdom, and in France. We may begin by looking at the interactions between the entertainment industry and defence and security institutions such as the Pentagon, the CIA, and MI6. Many historical and comparative approaches see works of popular culture as sites where ideology is projected, and denounce the political orientations of movies and series, which are thought to be subservient to the militaristic and imperialist logic of the United States.[18] These approaches ignore the specificity and realism of the televisual medium, and they seek above all to explain how Hollywood serves US national war policy.

A new genre of series emerged in 2001 in the wake of the mass attacks on New York and Washington (which happened to coincide with the launch of the major security series *24*, although the show had been shot well before them). Security series pose the question of the relation between reality and fiction directly: in the case of *24* and, later, *Homeland* it is not the 'real' that influences fiction, but rather 'reality' and 'fiction' mutually structure one another, co-determining each other.

In France, the United Kingdom, Denmark, Germany, the United States, and Israel, the number of films and series that reveal what happens 'behind the scenes' of democratic regimes facing terrorist threats is increasing significantly: *Hatufim, Homeland, The Bureau, The Looming Tower, Fauda, False Flag*, and *Deutschland 83, 86, 89*, are examples. The parallel development of post-apocalyptic series both indicates and increases awareness of the risks of environmental catastrophes and global conflict, as well as of a loss of values. These works and themes do of course reveal a moral state of the world, and can be analysed as mirrors or symptoms of societies.[19] But they can also be understood as tools of education, creativity, perfecting, and care, as part of a kind of soft power that must be examined, criticized, and understood in order to constitute a resource for public and cultural policy, especially if they are produced in connection with institutions (of health, of intelligence, of culture), a practice that opens innovative perspectives and also creates a certain number of risks (of influence, propaganda, and others).

The political and ethical dimensions of this corpus of TV series are undeniable, and their pedagogical value can also be explored—for example, around various themes central to politics today: discrimination, violence, terrorism, intelligence, and so on. The Israeli series *Fauda*, which presents an unvarnished view of a group of undercover Israeli anti-terrorist agents in the occupied territories—is watched and appreciated both in Israel and in Palestine, as well as across the Middle East, even though the last seasons are more controversial and more obviously close to Israeli governmental politics. The question of terrorism resonates differently depending on whether one is in France, the United Kingdom, or Israel; similarly, questions of gender and race are raised in different ways in different countries. Beyond playing an educational role, these series create the possibility of a shared dialogue.

Let us also note the marked increase in female characters in series, the evolution of representations of femininity and heroism, and the impact that these representations can have on structuring gender relations. Series that focus on counter-terrorism have played a crucial role in this, and now feature an increasing number of female agents—*Homeland*, of course, with the surprising Carrie Mathison, and the strong female characters on the otherwise rather masculine series *The Bureau*. In general, security series have pioneered the emergence of unique heroines, beginning with Sydney Bristow on *Alias*—an actor and a character who, it turns out, helped the CIA to recruit new agents, by making the agency look more attractive.

In contrast to existing analyses, I am not interested in understanding how series might mirror or be the symptom of a certain political climate. Instead, I focus on asking what the impact of these serial fictions may be on democratic regimes, including their capacity to serve as spaces of deliberation and contestation, as spaces where conflicts can be framed and claims publicly staked. Public fictions provide strong points of common cultural reference, filling ordinary conversations and political debates. More than simple entertainment, they make it possible to examine the links between individuals and communities within shifting political contexts. As I have noted, the widespread distribution of American series has made it possible to draw attention to numerous social, health, political, racial, and security issues. The revolution in narrative practices in the twentieth century, which was accompanied by true inventiveness on the part of creators, led to a change in the moral ambition of series, making it possible for them to tackle political and geopolitical issues. It has also widened the scope of productions beyond the United States, making it possible to account for a diversity of political situations. After the Israeli series that truly created the genre (*Hatufim*), we may note the quality and originality of European political series such as the Danish *Borgen*, the French

The Bureau, the German *Deutschland 1983, 1986*, and *1989* and the Spanish *La Casa de Papel*. It is as if the genre of political and security series presents an opportunity to challenge American domination of television series, so that other democracies can make their own political proposals.

It is certainly not my intent to go so far as to propose that we develop ways for series to influence decision-making processes or to have an effect beyond their moral power, but one may attempt—as I have done in my analyses of the security genre (a number of the columns collected in the companion volume *TV-Philosophy in Action* were written around the time of the 2015 terrorist attacks in France)—to take into account the powers of popular fiction in analyses and perceptions of terrorist violence, in the transmission and sharing of meanings and values, and thus of means of resistance. It is a matter of understanding how cultural objects that until recently were considered negligeable or pure entertainment can have such an impact on the public as well as on political and defence actors. This leads to taking into account and demonstrating their reflexivity, while also reconsidering the question of realism—not in terms of verisimilitude or resemblance to reality, but rather impact and action on 'the real'. This again makes it possible—within the context of a subject that is of course very delicate—to modify the political and cultural perspective on popular culture. Indeed, if we accept that it is not an 'inferior' or alienating version of culture, but rather a culture that generates common values that can be taken up through the circulation and discussion of material that is available to all and integrated into daily life, then it has a preventative or educational value that must be analysed.

Another important concept for studying TV series such as *Homeland* or *The Bureau* that deal with conflicts between ethics and politics, is that of point of view. By this I mean both point of view in the literal sense—since the placement and technical settings of the camera, in conjunction with a show's editing, assign the viewer a point of experience—and in the figurative sense, since the series' virtual topography influences the opinion or judgement the viewer will have of the situation thus presented. Other factors must also be taken into account: the performance of the actors; viewers' attachments to characters with whom they have regular contact over the long span of the series; the polyphony that makes it possible to understand multiple perspectives or to take an interest in a character initially perceived as an 'enemy' or as inscrutable, as on *24*, *Homeland*, *The Bureau*, and *The State*. Here again a logic of empowerment is at play, allowing the viewer to 'benefit' and to perfect themselves within a domain that few are really familiar with.

In such cases, it is no longer fitting to speak of 'reception', but rather of the usages of TV series, with all the agency and inventiveness in terms of forms of attachment to cultural objects that this supposes. Today, the entertainment industry's best-loved productions are 'matrices of intelligibility' that allow viewers to understand the world around them, as well as to demonstrate their creativity, through practices such as pastiche, summaries of imaginary episodes, reinventions of characters' arcs, criticism, and so on.

The new ambition we find in security series today parallels the kind of practical ethical reflection that has been defined as 'ordinary', and which is anchored in attention to the particularities of human situations and personalities. This is obvious on series such as *24*, *Fauda*, and most impressively on *The Looming Tower*. Security series thus paradoxically make possible the emergence of a heterodox ethics that constitutes a true alternative to mainstream ethics, which, with its focus on decisions and behaviours, remains removed from both everyday and political realities.[20]

Studying security series requires particular resources in moral philosophy and ethics. This is true of all series, but it is especially so for this corpus. It is no longer a 'liberal' or normative ethics that is required, but rather an ethics anchored in values, vulnerability, and care. It is not surprising that several of these series have featured the emergence of major female characters within a context dominated by men: Chloé O'Brien (Marylin Rajksub) on *24*, Carrie Mathison (Claire Danes) on *Homeland*, Marie-Jeanne Duthilleul (Florence Loiret-Caille) on *The Bureau*, and Hannah Wells (Maggie Q) on *Designated Survivor*.

Beyond the security genre, developing ethics rooted in case studies and particular situations (bioethics and medical ethics, ethics of care, ethics that focus on inequalities and vulnerabilities, questions of gender and sexuality, and new forms of life) is essential to reweaving the democratic fabric of societies. Such an effort also seeks to deepen the question of how one is educated into democracy, a question that today involves all sorts of new methods, with popular culture among them. TV series can be understood and analysed as performative discourses within ethics, politics, and aesthetics—as linguistic and cultural reference points that structure our understandings of the world and the experiences we have of it at both the individual and collective levels. Values and meanings are constantly transmitted, constructed, deduced, and invented by series and their audiences. Thus, they make it possible to examine the hitherto neglected question of a moral and political education through series, and of education into democracy, within a context in which processes of inclusion and the transmission of values have become problematic.

In various ways, the major series-producing countries—the United States, Italy, the United Kingdom, Israel, Denmark, Germany, and France—are today confronted with developments that threaten to weaken democracy and national unity (terrorist and religious violence, aging populations, widening inequalities, lack of space for the young, and for disagreement in general), making it necessary and urgent for them to develop new tools for democratic education. A comparative approach seems to be the right way to study a question loaded with prejudices on all sides. A philosophical approach to popular cinema and TV series can contribute to this education, which is so integral to democratic life and to the prevention of violence.

It has always been difficult for fans of a series to say goodbye, and for some, the recent end of two major shows has been one more disaster on top of the catastrophe of the pandemic. *The Bureau* is probably not over, but we have reached the end of the series as we knew and loved it, under the leadership of Eric Rochant, with his ever-endearing characters. *Homeland* ended quietly after eight seasons; in contrast, *The Bureau*—initially overlooked because of its arid and overly pedagogical style—is now lauded by critics and fans. However, the latter were not at all pleased with the last two episodes of season five, which Rochant entrusted to director Jacques Audiard, and they have expressed their indignation on social media.

This is reminiscent of the final season of *Game of Thrones*, which also sparked irritated commentary from fans; a sign not only of separation anxiety but also of viewers' attachment to the show, their appropriation of the characters and their trajectories—characters who were so much a part of fans' lives that they felt as if they knew them better than the creators who constructed this attachment in the first place. In this respect, the criticism that marked the series' final season and the many alternative endings fans proposed for it were the ultimate sign of the show's success. Similarly, the outcry from fans of *The Bureau* who cannot bear the break in style between the bulk of the series and its latest episodes, or who lament the fact that various characters have been abandoned mid-course (what will become of Pacemaker?) indicates the intensity of their relationship to the series and its heroes, constructed over the years, and to the very aesthetic of the show. This tendency of the audience to appropriate characters, to find it difficult to let go of them, to not know what will happen to them, is proof—if any were needed—of the extent to which TV series are part of our lives, especially when we have seen characters evolve and change, including physically, over the years.

Homeland and *The Bureau* are paradigmatic examples of the security genre, which was born in 2001: as mentioned earlier, the 9/11 attacks on New York and Washington happened to coincide with the release of the major series *24*. By presenting the constitutive stakes of a permanent state of insecurity, characterized by multiform threats and deterritorialized enemies, security series are not only sites onto which this new state of insecurity is projected, but are fully constitutive of it. In this way, security series directly raise the question of the relationship between reality and fiction. Even when they are fictional and dramatized, reality sometimes catches up with them. In the case of *Homeland*, it is not the 'real' that influences fiction, but rather reality and fiction co-determine one another. Thus, it is necessary to take into account and demonstrate their degree of reflexivity, while at the same time reconsidering the question of realism—understood not as a resemblance to reality, but rather in terms of impact and action on the real.

This unprecedented relationship between reality and fiction results, in part, from a revolution in how these series are made: connections between television professionals and security actors in the United States, the United Kingdom, and France (the Pentagon, the CIA, MI6, DGSE) have proliferated. The question is not how these series echo a certain political climate, but rather, conversely, what the impact of these series may be on democratic regimes, understood as spaces of deliberation and contestation, spaces where conflict is framed.

TV series provide strong common cultural referents, which populate both ordinary conversations and political debates. The revolution in narrative practices in the twenty-first century, which has gone along with true inventiveness on the part of series creators, has led to a change in the moral ambition of series. This has also allowed production to expand beyond the American classics. It seems that the security genre—and political series more broadly—represents an opportunity to challenge American dominance in television by multiplying political points of view and demanding more of the viewer. From the outset, it was the ambition of *The Bureau* to do better, and be truer, than *Homeland*.

By immersing us in specific worlds, security series, and other genres modify the viewer's experience: their virtual topography influences the viewer's opinion or judgement of the situations they present. Other factors are also at play: the actors' acting, the viewer's attachment to characters and frequent contact with them over the long duration of the series, the polyphony that makes it possible to hear diverging points of view and to become interested in a character initially perceived as an 'enemy' or as inscrutable. A logic of empowerment is at work here, allowing the viewer to perfect themselves within a context with which few are familiar, and to gain a better understanding of political situations. If we now miss *Homeland* or *The Bureau* it is as 'matrices of intelligibility' that allow their viewers to understand the world around them, as well as to demonstrate their own creativity (by creating pastiches, writing summaries of imaginary episodes, reinventing characters' trajectories, etc.). This ambition of security series has paralleled the practical ethical reflection that all series have developed—an 'ordinary' ethics, anchored in attention to the particularities of situations and human personalities, which we find at work in *24, Homeland, Fauda, The Bureau* and especially in *The Looming Tower*. These are traits shared by many important series, but security series make them into elements of political analysis.

Homeland, like *24*, proclaims itself fiction, and uses the audience's attachment to fictional characters to implicate us in political matters. But its role goes beyond creating a fictional universe that corresponds to global threats, beyond the topic of terrorism. The series has endeavoured not only to make the terrorist threat known and to remind us that the worst is always to come (a theme already taken up by *24*), but also to make us attentive to the invisible threat, rather than to highly visible signals, to teach us the always-alert gaze: the image of Carrie, in front of her surveillance screen, hypnotized by Brody's private life in the first episodes, is the most striking and disturbing image of the entire series, because it transforms the viewer, turning us all into spies, responsible for surveillance.

Homeland was the first indication that these series could begin to not only represent but also analyse foreign conflicts—and the role of the United States in them—in a new way. During its eight seasons, *Homeland* confronted its audience with a complex vision of global conflicts, a view of violence in the Middle East, as well as the American political violence that influenced and encouraged it.

Eric Rochant's *The Bureau* is exemplary of security series, and there is no doubt it is the best show in the genre. It takes a relatively distant point of view from its subject matter and has a pedagogical and documentary aspect. The show, no more than *Homeland*, is not a mirror of society, nor an ideological base for it, but rather a concrete and realist tool of democratic action by virtue of its educational value and the political and moral training it provides its audience, a task that it takes extremely seriously. From its first episode, the series has led the viewer step by step through the (fictional) operations of the DGSE and has clearly and expertly presented the dimensions of major geopolitical crises in the Middle East. The show's aesthetic and pedagogical ambition is also to anchor political analysis in the human: it is a series about 'human intelligence' (HUMINT). Thus, the latest seasons of *Homeland* and of *The Bureau* conclude with stories about double agents—an inexhaustible subject ever since Le Carré, but here updated for the Russia of today. And it is interesting that they all shift the focus to a new Russian enemy, as if leaving the post 9-11 Islamist threat.

One crucial concept that calls for further development in studying television series such as *Homeland* or *The Bureau* that deal with the conflict between ethics and politics is that of 'point of view'. Point of view literally, because the position and the technical settings of the camera, in combination with the editing, assign a point of experience to the viewer; figuratively, because this virtual topography influences the opinion or judgement they will have of the situation thus presented. Given the logic of empowerment at play in this genre, which allows the spectator to 'profit' and to perfect themselves in a field not well known to many, it is no longer appropriate to speak of reception but rather of the usage of television series, with all that this implies of agency and inventiveness in forms of attachment to a cultural object.

Like all series, but especially those in this corpus, the study of security series requires special resources in moral and ethical philosophy—no longer a liberal or normative ethics, but an ethics anchored in values, vulnerability, and care. Security series paradoxically allow the emergence of a heterodox ethics that constitutes a real alternative to mainstream ethics, which is based on decisions and behaviours, as far removed from everyday realities as from political realities. The alternative and context-based moral conceptions that are presented constitute the moral element of these public works and define the form of education that they inspire in the public. The question of a morality expressed by contemporary media, and of the educational potential of series, is therefore entangled in all dimensions of private and public life.

Democratic life presupposes not only a set of institutions, but also the education of each individual in recognizing and expressing their experience. Cinema and series give viewers new voices and self-confidence. By allowing us to grow and to enhance the intensity of our lives and our understanding of possibilities, films and TV series show us a democratic life that can be shared—through exchanges between equals and conversations about values that allow for the exploration of a collective form of life.

The training in democracy that series can provide represents a new reason for hope in a world where anti-democratic values have been promulgated by numerous political regimes. Series are sites of collective moral exploration and have been shown to constitute political resources at a time when democracies are at risk, but we have not really reflected on the role they might play—here again as a result of contempt for 'the popular'. As Ulysse Rabaté notes, it is indeed a matter of the 'democratization of perfectionism': 'Popular culture is a site for discussing the society in which we live, its norms and their possible transgression and liberation.'[21]

Recent attempts to implement educational programmes in morality and citizenship in France are doomed to fail because (among other reasons) they do not take into account inequalities in the transmission of culture, mechanisms of exclusion, and contexts of violence. It is thus urgent, at all levels of teaching, including university level, to think about the culture of citizenship beyond the traditional frameworks of moral education and by looking at its actual bases today—including those shared and shareable tools that series represent, whether they deal directly with current events (*The Bureau, Baron Noir, Fauda, The Looming Tower, The Comey Rule, Servant of the People*), or are more general in scope while still explicitly conveying democratic values (*Game of Thrones*)—without falling into moralism.

In *The Claim of Reason*, as mentioned before, Cavell defined philosophy as 'the education of grownups', in parallel with his ambition, in his writings on cinema, of giving popular culture (which for him primarily meant Hollywood movies) the function of changing us:

> In philosophizing, I have to bring my own language and life into imagination. What I require is a convening of my culture's criteria, in order to confront them with my words and life as I pursue them and as I may imagine them; and at the same time to confront my words and life as I pursue them with the life my culture's words may imagine for me: to confront the culture with itself, along the lines in which it meets in me.[22]

It thus becomes necessary to draw on Cavell's method in *Pursuits of Happiness*, where he provided magnificent analyses of seven classic Hollywood comedies using a method that can also be applied to the romantic comedies of the 1980s and 1990s, to disaster movies (which are often built around a remarriage structure), and to comedies and tragedies featuring homosexual couples (Ang Lee's *The Wedding Banquet*, 1993, and *Brokeback Mountain*, 2005, or Abdellatif Kechiche's *Blue Is the Warmest Color*, 2013) and finally, and overwhelmingly, to TV series, which are rarely constructed as remarriage plots (except, perhaps—and this is debatable—*The Leftovers, Dream On, The Americans*, or *The Affair*), but which are filled with perfectionist callings, with the desire to go beyond oneself.

What is meant by popular culture is no longer exactly popular in the sense of certain popular arts, even if it sometimes draws on the resources of those arts. Rather, the expression refers to shared culture that is generative of shared values, and which is the site of 'the education of grownups', who through it attain a form of self-education, cultivation of the self. It is in this sense that, for Warshow and for Cavell, cinema is at the heart of popular culture and the stakes of its criticism: 'Such a criticism finds its best opportunity in the movies, which are the most highly developed and most engrossing of the popular arts, and which seem to have an almost unlimited power to absorb and transform the discordant elements of our fragmented culture.'[23]

Pursuits of Happiness has influenced various writers, creators, and viewers (including philosophers, sociologists, filmmakers, movie critics, movie lovers, fans of American comedies, and fans of TV series), and this influence is today clearer than ever, now that importance is attached not only to the viewer's reception (a word that we are coming to understand to mean nothing), but also to their agency, the capacities they mobilize in watching. In his first work on cinema, *The World Viewed*, Cavell took as his starting point the popular nature of cinema, connecting it to a certain relationship to ordinary life, an intimacy with the ordinary: cinema is part of the movie lover's ordinary life. In a wonderful essay on the ontology of cinema in Cavell, Emmanuel Bourdieu defined the realism of cinema in terms of how it is ingrained in everyday life: 'Cinema is common and ordinary aesthetic experience; shared, involved, and intertwined with everyday life: a movie before or after dinner; returning home and perhaps spending the night dreaming of it, thinking about it at breakfast the next morning, etc.'[24]

It is as experience and not as object that cinema interests us, and this is the basis of ordinary criticism of cinema. Understanding cinema's relationship to philosophy thus implies learning what it means to 'check one's experience', that is, to examine one's experience and 'let the object or the work of your interest teach you how to consider it'.[25] This means there is an inevitable circularity here, as Emerson pointed out. Having an experience requires trusting your experience. This is the crucial point of TV series, which teach each viewer to experience themselves in conversation with characters, something that requires finding the words to speak one's experience—one of Cavell's central themes: the will to find one's voice within one's history, in contrast to the temptation of inexpressiveness.[26] The possibility of having an experience is inseparable from the question of expression; the possibilities, which cinema explores, of the natural expressiveness of human beings. This discovery, rooted in a reading of Wittgenstein, is the approach to cinema favoured by Cavell, and is his point of entry into its different genres. The conversations we see in comedies of remarriage, more recent comedy movies, and comedic or dramatic series do not duplicate ordinary conversations but rather express a relationship to ordinary words: 'These film words thus declare their mimesis of ordinary words, words in daily conversation. A mastery of film writing and film making accordingly requires, for such films, a mastery of this mode of mimesis.'[27]

The fact that such conversations are not 'only' discourse or content, the fact that they involve what Cavell calls 'photogenesis'—the projection of living characters onto the screen to speak these words—shows that such conversations are only possible and only exist in cinema, and that they even constitute the experience of cinema and inscribe the ordinary nature of language into cinema; the fact that (talking) movies put us in the presence of a body and a voice, of ordinary language.

Getting back to the ordinary means regaining adequacy between our words and world, coming near to our experience. First cinema, and later series—where conversational expression is at the very heart of the experience—represent and perform language's hold over the real. *The Arrival* (Denis Villeneuve, 2016) does this in extraordinary fashion; as the main character is integrated into a new (extra-terrestrial) language, it radically changes her perception of reality. Beyond relativist reflections on language as creating a 'view of the world', *The Arrival*, through the genre of science fiction, suggests the reality of language as a form of life, while also reflecting on the powers of cinema.

From this perspective, it is not for the critic or philosopher to interpret, but rather to let the film say what it has to show, to hear what it says: its voice. For Cavell, cinema is a response to scepticism, to the loss of an experience that escapes the viewer, but it is not a way of recuperating an inaccessible experience, of regaining the world through the projection of the world. Rather, it is a way of recognizing loss, as Godard pointed out in his own fashion: the first words of his *Histoire(s) du cinéma 1988–98* are: 'Cinema began in black and white in order to mourn life.'[28] The paradox in the idea of a return to the ordinary is that we are returning to something we never had: just as *Twin Peaks: The Return*, Austin, and Wittgenstein bring us back to the ordinary—to a place where we have never been. The comedy of remarriage genre expresses this aspiration for a return to the ordinary—the acceptance of repetition, both the repetition of remarriage, as well as of daily life—which in these films is only possible through a death (the loss of the other and of the world) followed by a rebirth.

Scepticism, which expresses and dissimulates the loss of a natural proximity to the world, is the loss of natural expression, of conversation. It represents a moment in which we have lost the usage of words, have lost contact with experience and the words to speak it. To mean what one says, to overcome scepticism, would be to recognize our nature as speaking subjects and to accept ordinary expressiveness: to accept our condition as linguistic and finite beings; our condition, to quote Emerson, as 'victims of expression'.[29] Our experience as viewers of cinema stems from ordinary and shared culture, from our access to the 'physiognomy' of the ordinary. The idea that the highest culture is shared culture is one of the fundamental values defended by Cavell. He teaches us that an ordinary aesthetics of cinema must defend not the specificity of the individuals who create a work, nor the works in their singularity, but rather common aesthetic experience—for example, the experience of the movie viewer who goes to a movie less for its director than for the actors, whom they have seen and liked in earlier films, and whom they wish to see in a new incarnation ('the same again . . . only a little different', as Cary Grant says in his famous tirade from *The Awful Truth*, Leo McCarey, 1937)—which is also a way of exploring oneself.

Cavell's argument in *Pursuits of Happiness* is that comedies of remarriage represent, in a comic mode, the essential feature of scepticism—the fact that the human condition is separation, that one is irremediably distant from others and from the world—and that their heroes and heroines display the ability to overcome this state of doubt and separation and to find each other again. And the tool of their reunions is just what is threatened in scepticism: acknowledgement and conversation, of which comedies of remarriage offer unparalleled examples. Far from being an incidental or minor genre, the remarriage genre is the crucible in which the educational ambitions of cinema were forged.

What characterizes the experience of cinema is that it is simultaneously mysterious and ordinary. Here we touch on the innate finitude of the experience of a film, which is always repeatable but always limited. In spite of the new viewing modalities that have been available for the past several decades (videos, DVD, digital platforms, the Internet), the temporality of film is always that of finitude. There always comes a time when it is over, and this feeling is part of the experience of a movie, making it a type of ordinary experience of life. In Cavell's work, that which, in *The Claim of Reason*, was the tragic expression of scepticism becomes, through a reading of Emerson and Thoreau, a way of pacifying it—of domesticating it through acceptance of the everyday. According to Cavell, such acceptance can be read in Hollywood comedies of remarriage, which in his thought play a role equivalent to that of Emerson and Thoreau in terms of the discovery of moral perfectionism. If we lack the mode of perception that the everyday, the near, the low, and the familiar inspired in Emerson and Thoreau, says Cavell, we will be blind to certain aspects of cinema, to the sublime it contains in its portrayal of the everyday. Comedies of remarriage are thus comedies of the ordinary: the reunion of the initially separated couple is achieved through acknowledgement of the everyday, through comic acceptance of finitude and repetition. And thus, *Pursuits of Happiness*, with its title that makes reference to the Declaration of Independence, is a book about morality. In it, Cavell teaches us that films and series can present moral content and teachings, and may do so as well as or better than the arguments of moral philosophy—without that content being in any way hidden or 'implied'. This illustrates the position that Diamond would later go on to defend regarding the relationship that literary works such as those of Henry James and Jane Austen can have to moral thought:

> Besides showing us the possibility and attractiveness of that view of human nature, such literature can lead us to a rejection of the heavy-handed, sententious, or solemn in moral thought; we see that the seriousness and depth of moral thinking is entirely independent of

> any earnest or moralizing tone . . . The appeal of such a view is to
> the intelligence of the reader, inviting him, as it does, to give moral
> thought, moral criticism, a place in an ideal of civilized human life.[30]

The immanent perspective on popular film that Cavell introduced is more than valid for TV series and for everything that involves the exploration and mixing of genres or the creation of a specific universe that is based on, and generative of, its own culture (the cult series *Buffy* is an example of this, as is the *Twin Peaks* universe). Cinema is important because of the place it has in our lives, because of its exploration of genres, and because of its capacity to absorb and produce fragments of our experience, an essential dimension of popular culture that ordinary criticism must take into account. Bourdieu explains that one of the specificities of cinema is its internal reference to genres, which is a specific modality of its investigation into its own expressive potentialities. Other arts appeal to the notion of genre, but do so retrospectively, in order to classify past works or to distinguish between them within a genre. In contrast, movies and series only exist within genres, and this is what defines them as popular: there is no essence of cinema and no mystique of the auteur. The model of the self-made viewer, which is integral to the development of popular culture, stands in contrast to aristocratic distinction: such a viewer constitutes their taste through their choice of favourite genres—action movies, romantic comedies, Westerns, science fiction, vulgar comedies for teens, vampire movies, and so on. TV series are the genre of the twenty-first century, although this genre can be broken down into major genres that constantly overlap and intersect: medical/romantic, Western/sci-fi, detective/metaphysical.

For Cavell, the constitution of genres and their importance is based on a particular property of how movies are made: that is, collectively. The production of a cinematic work is an enterprise that mobilizes not only a film's crew, led by its director, but also the entire community of other filmmakers and their works, since members of one team are likely to participate in or have participated in other movies made by the community in question:

> Henceforth, the system of reference in relation to which a work of
> art was formerly understood—that is, its author and its unique
> inspiration—dissolves. To understand a cinematic work, a system of
> reference must be found that transcends individual wills and inspi-
> rations. This system of reference is the collectively constituted genre.[31]

Beyond TV series, the creativity of genre is what drives the creation of a work of popular culture. For example, *The Philadelphia Story* could easily have ended with the marriage of the heroine and James Stewart's character, given how seductive he is (to her and to the viewer), but, as Cavell notes, the genre dictates otherwise—just as it does in Spielberg's *War of the Worlds*, where we don't even need to see the ending to know what happens. The remarriage genre continues to offer stories and solutions to contemporary cinema (here we may think of Kubrick's *Eyes Wide Shut*, 1999, or Jacques Audiard's *Rust and Bone*, 2012), and serves, in particular, as the backbone of disaster movies. For ordinary criticism, this means giving up on the retrospective and abstract constitution of genres and recognizing instead the role that reference to genres plays in organizing collective creation. Thus, it is important to take into account not only those models thought to be 'noble', or to have high cultural legitimacy (e.g., the ballroom scene in Visconti's *The Leopard*, 1963), but also those considered common (e.g. the dance shared by John Travolta and Uma Thurman in Quentin Tarantino's *Pulp Fiction*, 1995), or even vulgar. Cinema is filled with explicit references to archetypal works and to the genres it helps create in a given period. It is a question of what criteria define a 'good' movie, and criticism has often made it its job to come up with these, rather than letting them emerge in an immanent manner from the experience of films. Cavell's approach is markedly different from that of other philosophers of film,[32] which generally consists in describing the medium's essential properties in order to prescribe its possibilities and possible genres. In contrast, Cavell advocates analysing certain works or genres in order to pragmatically describe the possibilities of the medium. Similarly, according to Wittgenstein there is no 'essence of language' that would prescribe its norms or uses, nor any definitions of our concepts that would determine their future application.

In 'The Fact of Television', Cavell, employing the terminology of *The World Viewed*, posed a question: what is this medium's material basis? And we must return to this question and to *The World Viewed*. Movie masterpieces are those individual works that most fully reveal and acknowledge the conditions of the film medium, *The World Viewed* argues. There is no definition of film. As Victor Perkins explains:

> I do not believe that the film (or any other medium) has an essence which we can usefully invoke to justify our criteria. We do not deduce the standards relevant to Rembrandt from the essence of paint; nor does the nature of words impose a method of judging ballads and novels. Standards of judgment cannot be appropriate to a medium as such but only to particular ways of exploiting its opportunities. That is why the concept of the cinematic, presented in terms of demands, has stunted the useful growth of film theory.[33]

Cavellian genres are thus a posteriori reconstructions of structures that first function in practice and which are defined relative to a certain body of actual works—for example, a set of comedies produced during a given time period (the 1930s and 1940s) within a certain structure of production (the major Hollywood studios of the time). The structure of relatively invariable traits that Cavell describes under the name 'remarriage comedy' is not normative, because genre has no existence or definition outside a series of archetypal films. The expressive potentialities of cinema as aesthetic medium are created by their instantiation, by their actualization within a body of works that give them meaning and make them 'real possibilities'.

What are often called the (technical) potentials of the medium are not even possibilities until they are given meaning within a particular work. Thus, a cinematic genre is not a principle for after-the-fact classification, nor a normative system, but a creative force. This generative potential is an even better characterization of series, which demonstrate their own momentum and force when they continue beyond their original source material: for example, the second and third seasons of *The Handmaid's Tale* were not based on the book, and *Game of Thrones* went on well after the point where George R.R. Martin's saga left off, thanks to the sheer force of the characters.

Thus, none of the traits that appear in the definition of a genre is a necessary and sufficient connection for belonging to it, for the list of characteristic traits is entirely open, like the possible uses of a word in Wittgenstein. And the absence of a characteristic trait in a given genre (e.g., the absence of the heroine's mother in comedies of remarriage) can always be made up by a compensatory circumstance. It is true that belonging to the remarriage category would seem to presuppose a female heroine on a perfectionist quest, with the movie's starting point being her divorce or something similar, and its endpoint being (something like) her remarriage. But this structure does not constitute a set of necessary and sufficient properties for categorizing a work as part of the genre, and the list of properties defining the scope of a genre is never complete.[34]

The openness of a genre and its creativity allows for its later productivity, including in the derivation of new genres: the perfectionist quest in the genre of melodrama; remarriage or the equivalent (reconciliation/conversation) in romantic comedies; mutual education in comedies for teens such as *Knocked Up* (Judd Apatow, 2007). TV series have clearly inherited the conversational capacities of couples in classic Hollywood movies, which have provided series with the grammar of their expressions and interactions, as well as of their emotions. Thus, there is in genre a dimension of empowerment for later generations of characters. In the seemingly banal comedy *The Holiday* (Nancy Meyers, 2007), genre plays a determining role, allowing the heroine of one of its plotlines (Kate Winslet's character, who discovers comedies of remarriage during a vacation in California, at which time she also meets an old screenwriter and a young composer), to find the strength to reject her toxic ex and to express a new-found confidence in herself. Clips from these movies—including *The Lady Eve* (Preston Sturges, 1941) and *His Girl Friday* (Howard Hawks, 1940) are scattered throughout *The Holiday*, emphasizing this heritage and the fertility of the genre. Genre provides an expressive grammar, including for the viewer, who finds resources within it, just like Winslet's character, who draws on a genre to help navigate her own feelings and situation. This ordinary pedagogical dimension has become more radical with TV series, which are explicitly fields of ordinary expression.

They themselves are nourished by moments of conversation from recent or classic works, which make up their referential and moral universes—for example, the frequent allusions to TV or movie characters on *Lost* or *How I Met Your Mother* or *Girls*. A viewer's knowledge, or mastery, of a genre gives them a kind of ordinary competence that is a capacity for expression. Again, genre is not an essence, but rather the expressive possibilities opened up for actors and viewers alike. Thus, the comedy of remarriage genre proposes a grammar of moral education, which Cavell elaborated on in *Cities of Words*. The democratic nature of cinema lies in this capacity for education. Cavell declared his perplexity in the face of a question he was often asked: how is it that a professor of philosophy gets to thinking about Hollywood movies? For him, the question was backwards: 'For most of my life the opposite direction of the question would have been more natural: How is it that someone whose education was as formed by going to the movies as by reading books, gets to thinking about philosophy professionally?'[35] This is indeed the question, which arises again in Cavell's autobiography *Little Did I Know*: how can we come to find, in philosophy, satisfaction for the form of sensibility that we have developed, often beginning in childhood, by going to the movies? In other words, how is it that we might find in philosophy a form of satisfaction, of excitement, and of education, that converges with our interest in movies? We recognize the interest we have in movies in our interest in philosophy, and in our desire to be interesting. Cavell's directive is in no way an invitation to narcissism; rather, it is a moral obligation.

This also gives us an understanding that in order to arrive at and practise philosophy that would satisfy the cinephile, philosophy must be transformed: it must become something particular, unique. Philosophy must become akin to the kind of self-education that cinema provides: as Cavell notes, movies show us the important moments when life changes imperceptibly—moments that, in our actual lives, are fleeting and indeterminate, or whose importance it takes us years or an entire lifetime to understand. From this point of view, *Eternal Sunshine of the Spotless Mind* (Michel Gondry, 2004) is not only a reprise of comedies of remarriage, but also of *It's a Wonderful Life* (Frank Capra, 1946). In Gondry's movie, the horror lies not in seeing a world in which I do not exist, but rather a world in which the other does not exist, and from which I thereby also disappear. Just like Capra's movie, it is a reflection on (or by) cinema insofar as it projects the experience of loss,[36] loss of the world and of our own experience as it is constituted by fragments and memories, made up of images that count for us but have faded, like a colour that has lost its brightness.

The wonderful series *The Affair*, which presents us with different points of view (sometimes in intimate detail) on the same love story—showing first the viewpoints of the two main characters, whose encounter transforms the lives of many other people, and then widening out to include those of other characters—is also a reflection on TV series themselves. Rather than a plurality of points of view à la *Rashomon* (Akira Kurosawa, 1951), what

The Affair shows us are the memories of those who lived the story. It is a matter of educating one's own experience, not only in the classical sense of training one's aesthetic taste, but also in the sense of moral formation, and of the constitution of one's own singularity, which is never so operative as in one's choice of movies and moments. The ordinary nature of popular culture emerges in our capacity, as men and women who create ourselves out of the diversity of cultural offerings, to define our uniqueness and our morality through our choices in this domain.

This is the meaning of Cavell's emphasis on the experience of cinema, on 'the persistent exercise of your own taste, and hence the willingness to challenge your taste as it stands, to form your own artistic conscience, hence nowhere but in the details of your own encounter with specific works'.[37] Here, the ultimate stakes of his essay 'The Thought of Movies' emerge: knowing what is important, what matters for us. In *Pursuits of Happiness*, he proclaimed 'the importance of importance'. It is not only truth that is important, but also importance well; or rather, truth is defined by what is important, by what matters. This priority of the important, of mattering, over the beautiful and the true as concepts governing ordinary experience is the heart of ordinary culture. Why, indeed, do we remember a certain moment from a movie or series? Because of its importance to us, which stands in contrast to our lack of perception of importance in ordinary life, where it is inherently hidden:

> If it is part of the grain of film to magnify the feeling and meaning of a moment, it is equally part of it to counter this tendency, and instead to acknowledge the fateful fact of a human life that the significance of its moments is ordinarily not given with the moments as they are lived so that to determine the significant crossroads of a life may be the work of a lifetime. It is as if an inherent concealment of significance, as much as its revelation, were part of the governing force of what we mean by film acting and film directing and film viewing.[38]

Notes

1   Sandra Laugier, 'Vertus ordinaires des cultures populaires', *Critique* 776–77, no. 1 (2012): 48–61.

2   See Cavell, *Pursuits of Happiness*.

3   Cavell, *Claim of Reason*, p. 125.

4   Moral perfectionism is a heterodox ethics that focuses on transformation of the self, in contrast to classical ethics that is based on duty or rational choice. See Cavell, *Conditions Handsome and Unhandsome* (Chicago: University of Chicago Press, 1990) and Rothman, *Tuitions and Intuitions*.

5   See also Laugier, *TV-Philosophy in Action* (2023), in this series; as well as Robert Sinnerbrink's *Cinematic Ethics: Exploring Ethical Experience through Film* (London; New York: Routledge, 2016).

6   Cavell, *The World Viewed*, pp. 5–6.

7   Erwin Panofsky, 'Style and Medium in the Moving Pictures', cited in Cavell, *The World Viewed*, p. 30.

8   Cavell, *Pursuits of Happiness*, p. 12.

9   Ibid., p. 10.

10 Stanley Cavell, 'The Good of Film', in *Cavell on Film*, edited by William Rothman (New York: SUNY Press, 2005), p. 340.

11 Cavell, Epilogue to Warshow, *The Immediate Experience*, p. 292.

12 Ludwig Wittgenstein, *Philosophical Investigations*, translated by G.E.M. Anscombe (Englewood Cliffs, NJ: Prentice Hall, 1958), §118.

13 Stanley Cavell, *Little Did I Know: Excerpts from Memory* (Stanford, CA: Stanford University Press, 2010).

14 Cavell, Epilogue to Warshow, *The Immediate Experience*, p. 292 (emphasis added).

15 This ordinary understanding of politics is developed in Ogien and Laugier, *Pourquoi désobéir en démocratie* and *Le Principe démocratie*.

16 Chalvon-Demersay, 'La confusion' and 'Enquête'; Hervé Glévarec, *La sériephilie: sociologie d'un attachement culturel et place de la fiction dans la vie des jeunes adultes* (Paris: Ellipses, 2012).

17 Dominique Pasquier, 'La 'culture populaire' à l'épreuve des débats sociologiques', *Hermès, La Revue* 42, no. 2 (2005): 60–69.

18 David L. Robb, *Operation Hollywood: How the Pentagon Shapes and Censors the Movies* (Amherst, NY: Prometheus Books, 2004); Carl Boggs and Tom Pollard, *The Hollywood War Machine: U.S. Militarism and Popular Culture* (New York: Routledge, 2017; Tricia Jenkins, *The CIA in Hollywood: How the Agency Shapes Film and Television* (Austin: University of Texas Press, 2016).

19 See the European Research Council project *Demoseries* (2020–2024).

20 See Laugier, *Éthique, littérature, vie humaine*; Patricia Paperman and Sandra Laugier (eds), *Le Souci des autres: éthique et politique du care* (Paris: Éditions de l'Écoles des hautes études en sciences sociales, 2005), Laugier, *Politics of the Ordinary: Care, Ethics, Forms of Life* (Leuven: Peeters Publishers, 2020).

21 Interview with Ulysse Rabaté and Pierre Saint-Gal by Leo Rosell and Lenny Benbara, 7 October 2018, 'Le football traditionnel est indissociable du monde amateur' [translated from the French original], https://lvsl.fr/le-football-professionnel-est-in-dissociable-du-monde-amateur-entretien-avec-ulysse-rabate-et-pierre-saint-gal/.

22 Cavell, *Claim of Reason*, p. 125.

23 Warshow, *The Immediate Experience*, p. xxxviii.

24 Emmanuel Bourdieu, 'Stanley Cavell—Pour une esthétique d'un art impur', in *Stanley Cavell: Cinema et philosophie*, edited by Marc Cerisuelo and Sandra Laugier (Paris: Presses de la Sorbonne Nouvelle, 2001), p. 57 [translated from the French original].

25 Cavell, *Pursuits of Happiness*, p. 10.

26 I expand on this idea in Sandra Laugier, *Wittgenstein: le mythe de l'inexpressivité* (Paris: Vrin, 2010) and *Wittgenstein: politique de l'ordinaire* (Paris: Vrin, 2021).

27 Cavell, *Pursuits of Happiness*, p. 11.

28 Jean-Luc Godard, *Histoire(s) du cinéma* (Artificial Eye, 1988).

29 Emerson, 'Experience', in *Essential Writings*, p. 317. See Rothman, 'Justifying *Justified*', in *Television with Stanley Cavell in Mind*, edited by David LaRocca and Sandra Laugier (Exeter: University of Exeter Press, 2023), pp. 31–49.

30 Diamond, *The Realistic Spirit*, pp. 300–301.

31   Bourdieu, 'Stanley Cavell—Pour une esthétique d'un art impur' [translated from the French original].
32   See the classic work by Stephen Mulhall, *On Film* (London: Routledge, 2001).
33   Victor F. Perkins, *Film as Film: Understanding and Judging Movies* (Harmondsworth and New York: Penguin Books, 1972), p. 59. See also Rothman, 'Justifying *Justified*'.
34   See Wittgenstein's concept of family resemblance, and Chapter 3.
35   Cavell, 'The Thought of Movies', in *Cavell on Film*, p. 88.
36   See Marc Cerisuelo, 'Le cinema change en sa perte', in *Stanley Cavell: Cinéma et philosophie*.
37   Cavell, 'The Thought of Movies', in *Cavell on Film*, 93.
38   Ibid.

3

Family Resemblances

Let us return to the question of the ontology of series. If there are no artistic masterpieces among television's individual works, as 'The Fact of Television' argues, then 'what is memorable, treasurable, criticizable',[1] what reveals or acknowledges the television medium, must reside not in a programme's individual episodes, but in the programme 'as such', what Cavell calls its format. In an (old-style) series, in Cavell's sense, every episode tells a complete story that begins when a baseline of normality, the realm of the everyday, the ordinary—a crucial concept for Cavell—is disrupted by a crisis and ends with the crisis being resolved and a return to normality. In this respect, the format is a formula for generating a programme's individual instances. By contrast, in a movie genre such as the comedy of remarriage, what we might think of as the formula—what *Pursuits of Happiness* calls the genre's myth— is reinterpreted and revised by each member of the genre. The formula doesn't generate the instances; the instances generate the formula.

The idea of genre and of medium is central to any aesthetic rehabilitation of TV series. 'The Fact of Television' takes up the ontology of *The World Viewed* by defining the material basis of the medium of television—apart from which there would be nothing we could call television—as 'a current of *simultaneous event reception*'.[2] Each of these words registers a significant difference between film and television, for *The World Viewed* defined the material basis of the medium of film as 'a succession of automatic world projections'.[3] 'The mode of perception that I claim is called upon by film's material basis is what I call viewing. The mode of perception I wish to think about in connection with television's material basis is that of *monitoring*.'[4]

'A current of simultaneous event reception' is the material basis for all television formats, and also for all the formats and the individual programmes that those formats support. Beyond this, television is itself a format, at once one kind of 'current of simultaneous event reception' (radio is another) and an instance of such a current. (We can say that television is a current of simultaneous event reception; we cannot say that film is a succession of automatic world projections.) Cavell goes on to reflect, in a prescient passage, on ways in which our sense of what television is might be affected by future technological developments: 'If the distribution of videocassette recorders and cable television increases, as appears to be happening, to the size of the distribution of television itself, or to a size capable of challenging it, this will make problematic whether television will continue to exist primarily as a medium of *broadcasting*.'[5] The change that this passage anticipates had largely come to pass in 1988, when Cavell published another essay, 'The Advent of Videos', in which he returned to a thought he had expressed in 'The Fact of Television':

> If the increasing distribution of videocassettes and disks goes so far as to make the history of film as much a part of the present experience of film as the history of the other arts is part of their present—hence, in this dimension, brings film into the condition of art—it will make less respectable the assumption of the evanescence of the individual movie, its exhaustion under one viewing, or always casual viewings.[6]

In 'The Advent of Videos',[7] Cavell considers some implications of the fact that in the time since he had published 'The Fact of Television', this, too, had come to pass. The assumption of 'the evanescence of the individual movie', as Cavell put it, was a repression of film as an art, and also of the specificity of this art. Cavell's thinking about film led him to 'recognize the need for prose capable of evoking the evanescence of the world on film, the ever-shifting moods of "faces and motions and settings," and capable of capturing, as well, what remains inflexible, fixed, in the physiognomy of the world on film ... the "unmoving ground" that makes film capable of exhibiting the world'.[8] Film studies has to acknowledge 'the double existence—the transience and permanence—that is automatically possessed by the world on film, vouchsafed by the ontological conditions of the medium'.[9]

By 1988, the proliferation of video cassette recorders and video stores had for the first time made readily available the corpus of great works that have shaped film's history as an art. When Cavell wrote *The World Viewed*, he had to rely on his memories of movies that had become 'strand over strand' with memories of his life. As he puts it in *Pursuits of Happiness*:

> People bear these films in their experience as memorable public events, segments of the experiences, the memories, of a common life. So that the difficulty of assessing them is the same as the difficulty of assessing everyday experience, the difficulty of expressing oneself satisfactorily, of making oneself find the words for what one is specifically interested to say.[10]

When Cavell wrote *Pursuits of Happiness*, he could check his memories against the films themselves. The unprecedented availability of movies in forms that facilitated study made it possible for criticism to strengthen the medium and

changed our sense of what film *is*. The same can be said of television: the development of TV availability has changed the medium. Still, TV series are not as
available to us as a movie, that is, they need much more time and all viewers
know how hard it is to retrieve a scene or conversation or line or image that
"matters to us", as Cavell says about the moments that definie the "ontology"
of film. Somehow, we are back with series to Cavell's early method: we just have
to rely on our memories, on our experience: they are not readily available to us.

Whether I am watching a programme on a broadcast or cable channel,
I can be said to be watching television—the medium whose material basis
is 'a current of simultaneous event reception'. This is why in 'The Fact of
Television' Cavell could say that he does not regard broadcasting 'as essential
to the work of television'.[11] But if I am watching an episode I have taped, he
couldn't say I was watching television. Simultaneity is essential to television's
material basis, in Cavell's view. But VCRs and DVD players—and the same
holds for streaming video—eliminate simultaneity. What we are watching is
not a current of simultaneous event reception; it is not a current, much less a
simultaneous one, and there is no event being received. By Cavell's criteria, what
we are watching is not to be called television; or, if we do choose to refer to it
as television (as when we call a Netflix series a television series), this registers
that our sense of what television is has changed since Cavell wrote 'The Fact of
Television'. The ontology of television becomes ordinary language philosophy.[12]

No doubt, the experience of watching a movie streamed or played on a
VCR or DVD player differs in small and large ways from viewing a film
projected on a movie screen with an audience in a cinema. But our mode
of perception is still viewing, not monitoring. This is why the first season of
Homeland is so striking, for it enacts this difference: you see (on your screen)
Carrie watching and monitoring what is happening in Brody's house—'a
current of simultaneous event reception'.

In defining masterpieces of an art as those works that most meaningfully
reveal or acknowledge that art's material basis, 'The Fact of Television' relies
on concepts that figure centrally in *Must We Mean What We Say?* And *The
World Viewed*—concepts linked in those books to Cavell's reflections on the
modern. *Pursuits of Happiness* shifted the emphasis from *The World Viewed*'s
focus on what it means for something to be a film to what it means for a
film to be a comedy of remarriage—one artistic medium that film's material
basis supports. Although 'The Fact of Television' was written after *Pursuits of
Happiness*, its focus shifted back to the material basis of the medium as such:

> The question what becomes of objects when they are filmed and
> screened—like the question what becomes of particular people, and
> specific locales, and subjects and motifs when they are filmed by
> individual makers of film—has only one source of data for its answer,
> namely the appearance and significance of just those objects and
> people that are in fact to be found in the succession of films, or
> passages of films, that matter to us.[13]

The important moments in series are defined in light of the importance of moments from movies: they are the moments, episodes, or characters that matter to us. To explore such data, as in the philosophy of language, it is necessary to determine the nature of these appearances, of this significance, of that importance. There is, Cavell says, a kind of affinity between cinema—good movies—and a particular understanding of the good; an understanding that is foreign to, or underlies, dominant moral theories,[14] which can be subverted through such a definition. A good movie is one that allows us to know ourselves, to understand what we are interested in. The melodramas and comedies Cavell wrote about are examples of this. Such an understanding of the good is closer to perfectionist ethics (that is, an ethics of the education and elucidation of the self) than to normative ethics: 'As a perfectionism it is going to have something to do with being true to oneself, or, in Foucault's title, the caring of the self, hence with a dissatisfaction, sometimes despair, with the self as it stands.'[15]

From this perspective, morality is defined by individual claims and by recognition of the claims of others—that is, by a plurality of moral positions and voices within the same world, and the collective determination of what matters. These films constitute a laboratory for moral conversation, which today is continued in TV series.

And it is from this point of view that we may take up Cavell's particular method, which, in all his books on film, essentially consisted in basing himself on his memories of movies. It is a contestable, or at least strange, approach. Why not do a shot-by-shot analysis instead? To respond to this objection and to justify his method, Cavell explained that what interests him are 'the causes of my consciousness of films as it stands'.[16] In the experience of cinema, as in the usage of language, and as in the usage of series, the judgement and memories of each person have a claim to universality and to validity (and, for Cavell, such claims, which are inherent in the use of ordinary language, recall the claims made in aesthetic judgements):[17] 'We involve the movies in us. They become further fragments of what happens to me, further cards in the shuffle of my memory, with no telling what place in the future. Like childhood memories whose treasure no one else appreciates, whose content is nothing compared with their unspeakable importance for me.'[18] Read in the twenty-first century, this methodological point is the strongest link between the experience of film and TV. And it is paradoxical but illuminating that Cavell's apparent early criticism of the aesthetic value of TV works would be a powerful argument for the value and importance of the TV series experience, once a corpus of great TV has been established.

Cinema, as ordinary culture, has more to do with autobiography than with aesthetics. Its importance may well be completely unrelated to the established values of movie criticism when it sees itself as art criticism. When Cavell's book *The World Viewed* was published, Rosalind Krauss considered it an 'extreme curiosity' from the point of view of theoreticians of cinema, who were readers and admirers of Eisenstein, Vertov, Brakhage, and Warhol.[19]

According to Krauss, Cavell combined historical ignorance with an inability to distinguish between important—that is, experimental—cinema and entertainment that barely merits being called 'cinematic'. Cavell's redefinition of the important is the hallmark of his approach to popular culture and of his ordinary subversion of criticism. It also characterizes TV series.

In 'More of the World Viewed', which Cavell wrote several years after *The World Viewed*, he contests the possibility of determining the importance of a film from a solely theoretical or historical point of view.[20] As in the political realm, when it comes to movies or series, I alone can say what matters, can determine what is important and significant. This is the democracy of cinema. In my personal experience, *Titanic*, *Knocked Up*, and some of the *Star Wars* movies have mattered as much as any 'auteur' classic.

The perspective on ordinary culture that Cavell's work opened up makes it possible to perceive the moral importance of TV series, which arouse considerable interest in the intellectual world, but still have not found a critical discourse that can match the richness of their material and the creativity of the discipline. This has been because of a lack of resources on the part of those who take an interest in series, resources that would allow them to reconcile the moral education that comes from frequenting series and characters with their status as impassioned fans, and with the conceptual overstimulation created by the richness and variety of the material, which is characteristic of popular culture. Cavell's perspective on popular film, and this exigency for criticism, apply in my view to TV series as well, and to everything that has to do with exploring and mixing 'genres' of culture.

The success of TV series stems in particular from their polyphonic nature. They depict a plurality of singular expressions, portray disputes and debates, and are permeated by a moral atmosphere. The methodology and narrativity of series account for their moral relevance. But this inevitably leads to revising the status of morality, as well as to seeing it not in rules and principles of decision-making, but rather in attention to ordinary behaviour, to everyday micro-choices, to individuals' styles of expressing themselves and making claims. Various philosophers, weary of overly abstract meta-ethics, have already called for such transformations. The material of TV series allows for greater contextualization, historicity (regularity, duration), and familiarization, as well as an education of perception (attention to the expressions and gestures of characters we come to know; attachment to recurring figures who are integrated into everyday life; the presence of faces and words on the 'small screen').

This answers the question Cavell raised about the moral function of 'public' works and the form of education they inspire in the public and private worlds they create. The intertwining of the private and the public is also an intertwining of modes of constituting an audience. The address to an audience becomes the constitution of a public discourse and its norms. Morality is constituted by individual claims and by recognition of the claims of others, by recognizing a plurality of positions and moral voices within the same small world.

TV series rearticulate the private and the public differently from the darkened cinema:[21] they slip into domestic, private life. Understanding this requires taking seriously the moral intentions of the producers and screenwriters of TV series and TV movies, and the constraints thus imposed on them. This is again in line with Cavell's reading: breaking with a critical tradition that saw the intelligence and meaning of a film as a by-product of critical analysis, he affirmed the importance of the collective writing of films—and this is clearly true of series as well—and of the role of screenwriters and directors, as well as of actors and actresses, in developing the significance and educational value of a film.

For example, the vampire theme, which has become central in popular culture to the point that it now constitutes a genre of its own, makes possible the representation, democratization, and appropriation of essential moral questions about life and death, and facilitates the education (in particular the sexual education) of teens and adults more efficiently than any other genre. Here we may think of the importance for adolescent culture of the series *Buffy the Vampire Slayer*—whose heroine, Buffy, fell in love with two splendid vampires in a row (Angel and Spike; let's forget about the ridiculous Riley in season 4, please). *True Blood*, a series without equal, was able to subtly express and transmit anti-racist and anti-homophobic positions from the very beginning. Comedies for 'young people' such as *How I Met Your Mother*, which continues the tradition of *Friends* and *Buffy* (a significant number of actors from *Buffy* were featured in *How I Met Your Mother*), allow viewers to experience a range of ordinary situations in young adult life as part of various perfectionist journeys, as well as the different forms of expression that constitute their grammar and their solutions.

Despite the diversity of TV series, their writing is always based on the desire for a joint and public expression of despair and on the hope that new conversations will be born. These shows testify to hope in the educability of viewers, who are obliged to familiarize themselves, and gradually to train themselves, like children being integrated into a form of life, as described by Wittgenstein at the beginning of the *Philosophical Investigations*.

Series allow for a joint exploration of the ordinary form of life and human forms of life that recalls the articulation of the social and the biological in Wittgenstein's concept of *Lebensform*.[22] Great series are full of moments of description of the human form of life. For example, in the fifth season of *Buffy*, after the death of Buffy's mother, her friends enter a period of mourning during which Anya, Alex's girlfriend and a newcomer to the rites of human life, asks about their behaviours and about the meaning of the loss of a life. Or we may think of the kinds of explorations into what it is to be alive—or not—in vampire series and series focused on serial killers: *Dexter, Hannibal, Killing Eve*.

It is within popular culture, and particularly in movies and series, which have a special affinity with everyday life, that an access or mode of approach to the ordinary is constituted. As we know, for Cavell, cinema is not an aesthetic object but an ordinary practice, repeatable and integrated into our existences. Talking movies, in particular, are the projection of ordinary conversation and expression onto a screen; they are not recordings of ordinary conversations, but rather constitute ordinary conversations. This relationship to the ordinary is immediately visible in scenes from classic Hollywood movies in which the heroes share everyday moments: for example, when Clark Gable and Claudette Colbert act out a domestic scene in *It Happened One Night*, or the apocalyptic scene in *Woman of the Year* (George Stevens, 1942), in which Katharine Hepburn makes breakfast. Such moments show the domestication of scepticism by the everyday, without making the threat of it disappear. We know that the horror and fantasy genres correspond to a particular terror of the everyday—kitchen or bathroom utensils and appliances may turn deadly. Such ambivalence is characteristic of the everyday in cinema: the uncanniness of the ordinary emerges in classics such as *It's a Wonderful Life*, in which the hero (James Stewart) is presented with a world he is not a part of, revealing the sceptical structure of cinema itself—for it too presents us with successive projections of worlds in which, necessarily, we don't exist. As noted by Bourdieu, 'The distance that cinema establishes between its viewers and the projections of the world that comprise it reproduces the distance from the world itself that, as contingent creatures, our fundamental "foreignness" implies.'[23] Capra's *mise-en-scène* in the film plays on particular qualities of cinema—qualities it shares with our own experience of the world.

In recent popular culture, we may think of the final scene of *Gravity* (Alfonso Cuaron, 2013), which represents the terrestrial form of life in a unique way after its heroine's journey and return to earth: as the human fact of being subject to gravity, and hence to necessities. Disaster movies are often forceful and unexpected explorations of ordinary life insofar as it is threatened or destroyed, always defined by the absence of what has been or may be lost. *The Walking Dead* and *The Leftovers*—certainly the most interesting series of the 2010s—explore the relationship to the lost ordinary. Gondry's *Eternal Sunshine of the Spotless Mind* is a remarkable reflection on the medium's capacity to represent the loss of ordinary life (through the erasure of memories) and the possibility of regaining it through contact with others—in this case, through a remarriage, expressed by Jim Carrey's 'Okay' at the end of the movie.

Such memorable moments are favoured fragments of experience that will constitute a subjective grammar—the grammar of expressing importance:

> People bear these films in their experience as memorable public events, segments of the experiences, the memories, of a common life. So that the difficulty of assessing them is the same as the difficulty of assessing everyday experience, the difficulty of expressing oneself satisfactorily, of making oneself find the words for what one is specifically interested to say.[24]

It is in this respect that the ordinary creates a philosophy. In his book on Thoreau,[25] Cavell asked, provocatively, whether American philosophy exists. The answer is yes, and it proclaims itself in Emerson's words: 'I ask not for the great, the remote, the romantic; what is doing in Italy or Arabia, what is Greek art, or Provencal minstrelsy; I embrace the common, I explore and sit at the feet of the familiar, the low. [26]

Cavell's first point is that the specificity of American thought lies in its invention of the ordinary. His second is that this invention of the ordinary, which began with Emerson and Thoreau, is most fully realized in Hollywood cinema, the only common cultural reference in a culture too new to have or appreciate its own classics. From the beginning of his philosophical career, Cavell's motto was an expression borrowed from Wittgenstein: to bring words back from their metaphysical usage to their ordinary usage; to bring them home.[27] This return to ordinary usages does not imply bringing philosophy to an end, but rather reinventing it in a new category, in a new mode, or, to use one of Emerson's favourite terms, a new mood: that of the ordinary.

One of Cavell's earliest claims, from *Must We Mean What We Say?*, is that we do not know what we think or mean, and that philosophy's task is to bring us back to ourselves; to bring our words back to their everyday usage, to bring knowledge of the world back to knowledge of or proximity to the self. There is nothing easy or obvious about this, and the quest for the ordinary, for its expression and representation, is in fact the most difficult one there is, even if (and precisely because) the ordinary is right here, available to each and every one of us. The voice of the ordinary only takes on its full meaning in response to the risk of scepticism—that loss or distancing of the world, that loss of words that haunts the contemporary world and is the central theme of cinema, from Frank Capra to Terrence Malick.[28] The appeal to the ordinary is neither proof nor a solution; it is suffused with scepticism, with what could be called 'the uncanniness of the ordinary'—which is exactly what motivated the invention of cinema, and which David Lynch has explored in his films and series, perhaps more deeply than any other director. This desire to reach the ordinary is present in every cinematic image, where it produces an internal response to scepticism.[29]

Through their attention to the ordinary, the common, and the familiar, Emerson and Thoreau both herald and permeate the ordinary language philosophy of Wittgenstein and Austin and prepare the way for the invention of cinema and other popular cultures:

> The connection means that I see both developments—ordinary language philosophy and American transcendentalism—as responses to skepticism, to that anxiety about our human capacities as knowers that can be taken to open modern philosophy in Descartes, interpreted by that philosophy as our human subjection to doubt. My route to the connection lay at once in my tracing both the ordinary language

philosophers as well as the American transcendentalists to the Kantian insight that Reason dictates what we mean by a world.[30]

How do I know what *we* mean by a word or by a world? Emerson and Thoreau answer the question of the intimacy between words and the world with an exploration of the ordinary. It is this naturalness of ordinary language and conversation as a form of access to or contact with the world that Emerson allows us to regain in response to scepticism. There is clearly something surprising about this. How can writers as marginal to philosophical culture as Thoreau and Emerson measure up to philosophy as we know it, to either so-called continental or classical philosophy, or to analytic philosophy as it has so fruitfully developed in the United States since the mid-twentieth century? And how can film, or TV series, compete with philosophy? To discover the answer, one must truly take American thought and culture as a whole seriously: to accept that there is, in Shakespeare, in Capra, or in McCarey, a reflection on scepticism as radical as in any classical philosophical works, and, in general, to accept that, as Thoreau noted in *Walden*, many of the things we think we discover in the heavens of philosophy are in front of us or under our feet. Again, it is not a matter of being anti-philosophy or anti-theory—positions that are all too often attributed to Wittgenstein and Emerson. Nor is it a matter of 'pop philosophy'—a strange concept that implies some sort of amusing version of philosophy created at the expense of pop culture. Rather, it is a matter of reformulating philosophy, starting over. What has led me to consider TV series as a philosophical medium is that I have always sought to take Cavell's proposition seriously when, in *Pursuits of Happiness*, he compared *It Happened One Night* with the *Critique of Pure Reason*, thus showing the intimate relationship that unites cinema and philosophy in their representation and projection (or view) of the world:

> I am not insensible, whatever defenses I may deploy, of an avenue of outrageousness in considering Hollywood films in the light, from time to time, of major works of thought. My sense of the offense this can give came to a climax in presenting a draft of my essay on *It Happened One Night* to a university symposium entitled 'Intellect and Imagination: The Limits and Presuppositions of Intellectual Inquiry.' This essay begins with the longest consecutive piece of philosophical exposition in the book, concerning the thought of Immanuel Kant, whose teaching has claim to be regarded as the most serious philosophical achievement of the modern age. And what follows this beginning is the discussion of a Frank Capra film, not even something cinematically high-minded, something sad and boring, something foreign or foreign-looking, or something silent.[31]

Cavell saw his essay as performing 'a little transgression in its indecorous juxtaposition of subjects', but he was also seeking to test 'the limits or the density of what we may call our common cultural inheritance',[32] of which cinema is just as much a part as Kant is—perhaps more deeply in the United States than elsewhere. (I myself have experienced what it is like to commit such a 'transgression' when, in teaching university courses on philosophy, I have used popular movies and scenes from TV series to represent 'agreement in language' or other concepts from ordinary language philosophy.) Cavell mentions his perplexity when he was asked, during his talk, to first give a brief presentation of Kant, so that 'one unfamiliar with Kant' could understand the claims he made in his text—as if his essay were not a sufficient presentation of Kant, and as if he (or any other professional philosopher) could present Kant's argument in some kind of pure form, independently of any attempt to show what is interesting about it.

In rereading this, we realize that Cavell's contribution—and this is what makes it a powerful approach for reading series now, in the same way that he read Hollywood movies—was to show that the reality of the world and our approach to things are today formed by our experiences of ordinary art, and that, to quote Dewey, 'the sense we now have for essential characteristics of persons and objects is largely the *result* of art … If we are now aware of essential meanings, it is mainly because artists in all the various arts have extracted and expressed them in vivid and salient subject-matter of perception.'[33]

It might seem at least paradoxical that a medium such as cinema could constitute a response to scepticism and to the distancing of the world—that is, if Cavell had not shown in *Pursuits of Happiness* that Hollywood cinema took up the problem of scepticism where tragedy had left it. The comedies and melodramas Cavell studied are a 'laboratory' of moral exploration, and it is in them that morality is truly to be found. One must 'see in the laboratory of film the democratization of perfectionism … recognize what we are capable of in the undramatic, repetitive, daily confrontations to which they call attention'.[34]

Cavell's argument in *Pursuits of Happiness* is that comedies of remarriage represent, in a comic mode, the essential characteristic of scepticism—the fact that separation is the human condition, that I am irremediably distant from others and from the world—and that through their heroes and heroines, these movies depict the capacity to overcome this state of doubt and separation, to find oneself and one another again. The tool of such reunions is conversation, of which marriage comedies offer unparalleled examples. One iteration of scepticism is the impossibility of conversation, the impossibility of entering into a relationship with others through language; an impossibility that tragedy captures. Ordinary language is entirely permeated by this scepticism. Conversation is acceptance of the human linguistic condition, and thus constitutes the response to scepticism and to distance from the world.

The genius of Cavell is to have discovered that the solution to scepticism lies not in a refutation but in a 'turning'—what, in *The Claim of Reason*, he calls 'a turning of our natural reactions'.[35] Scepticism concludes that the human condition is separateness, that I am hopelessly distant from others and from the world. It is the avoidance of this conclusion that is ultimately fatal. How can this fatality be circumvented? Through the opposite of avoidance: acknowledgement. Cavell's idea, at once obvious and unprecedented, is to see comedy as a turning, a conversion of tragedy on the basis of the same data. In tragedy, the intolerable idea of separation is fatally avoided; in comedy, this inevitable state is not forgotten, but rather is happily accepted (or as happily as possible).

It is in American talking movies, and not the theatre, that the vision from Emerson's 'The American Scholar' is realized: that of an art that does not describe 'the great, the remote', but rather 'the familiar'; an art that comes back to ordinary existences and conversations in order to regain contact with the world, and, with it, proximity to the other. All this happened well after Emerson and Thoreau, who are nevertheless very much present in American cinema, from Capra and Douglas Sirk to more recent works. In particular, a strong Emersonian presence emanates from Spielberg's and Malick's respective war films (*Saving Private Ryan* and *The Thin Red* Line, both 1998).

The entire conceptual framework of *Pursuits of Happiness* shows that Shakespearian tragedy and the Hollywood comedies of remarriage of the 1930s share the same premise. Comedies of remarriage are closer to what Northrop Frye called 'Old Comedy' than to 'New Comedy', [36] since they focus on a heroine who undergoes the equivalent of death and rebirth. But one particularity of comedies of remarriage is that in them the heroine is a married woman, and the threat looming over her is not that of death (we are in a comic register after all), but rather divorce—the death of the marriage—which represents separateness. Here, the goal of the comedy is to reunite a separated couple (rather than to unite a young couple as in 'New Comedy'), by means of a process of acknowledgement. These reunions are made possible by a tool that is precisely what is threatened or denied in scepticism—that is, conversation, of which comedies of remarriage offer, within the euphoric atmosphere of the early era of 'talkies', unrivalled examples—just think of the conversations between Hepburn and Spencer Tracy in *Adam's Rib* (George Cukor, 1949), or Grant and Irene Dunne in *The Awful Truth*.

> Pervading each moment of the texture and mood of remarriage comedy is the mode of *conversation* that binds or sweeps together the principal pair ... Conversation is given a beautiful theory in John Milton's revolutionary tract to justify divorce, making the willingness for conversation (for a 'meet and happy conversation') the basis of marriage, even making conversation what I might call the *fact* of marriage.[37]

Conversation here is not theatrical banter, but rather a tool for acknowledgement and forgiveness, as well as the site where a relation of equality is invented, where education and recognition of the other are built.

Comedies of remarriage explore the same themes as *Othello* and *A Winter's Tale*—adultery, jealousy, fear of feminine sexuality, denial of acknowledgement—themes that Shakespeare's texts already made clear can always be converted, turned, from tragedy to farce (as in the first scene of *Othello*). Similarly, comedy constantly verges on tragedy, as shown by the melodramatic beginning of *Adam's Rib* (in which a woman shoots her unfaithful husband), as well as the scene in which Spencer Tracy's character threatens to kill himself with a revolver made of liquorice. Othello's jealousy is de-dramatized in the famous scenes from comedies of remarriage in which the hero (e.g., Cary Grant in *The Awful Truth* and *His Girl Friday*) must confront a rather ridiculous rival, thus beginning a long endeavour of acknowledging and accepting the other—his wife, from whom he had seemed to be irrevocably distant, and whom he learns to recognize as both an object and subject of desire. An emblematic example of such a scene is the improbable moment in *The Awful Truth* in which Dunne, pretending to be Grant's sister for the occasion, performs a sexual and vulgar rendering of a song heard earlier, 'My Dreams are Gone with the Wind', by the singer Dixie Belle—thus opening the path to their reconciliation, showing herself to be both close (similar) to him, and a million miles (different) from him. In *Trainwreck* (Judd Apatow, 2017), the heroine (Amy Schumer) appears before her boyfriend dressed as a cheerleader, completely disconcerting him, and performs a hit-and-miss demonstration of her talents, which, in this case too, leads to an improbable reconciliation. In both scenes, the stupefaction mixed with embarrassment and then desire expressed on the male character's face marks a transformation of values and a radical change that makes it possible to overcome the scepticism of the break.

Scepticism seems to erect a wall between beings and the world, or between humans and one another. Such a wall is also represented in comedies of remarriage—for example, the famous blanket ('the Walls of Jericho') in the motel room in *It Happened One Night*, or the swinging door that separates the couple in *The Awful Truth* (which is associated with the two separate doors through which the two figurines on the cuckoo clock enter and exit in the last scene). Both films end with the wall coming down: the blanket falls to the sound of a trumpet in *It Happened One Night* and the two figurines go back through the same door in *The Awful Truth*. Comedies of remarriage do not deny the separation of beings or their difference, as arguments against scepticism do; reconciliation entails acceptance of the state of separation and of difference, through a new paradigm—that of equality. Accepting the other means accepting being their equal, their peer, at once 'the same and different'. It means opening oneself to the intimate mixture that defines the 'meet and happy conversation' of marriage: friendship and amusement on the one hand, romance and sexuality on the other.

Such conversation can be found not only in the comedies Cavell discusses in *Pursuits of Happiness*, but also in the romantic comedies of the turn of the twenty-first century, recent comedies for teens, and, of course, comedy series such as *Friends* and *How I Met Your Mother*, as well as in all the conversational series that are rooted in conversation and collective exploration, including *Game of Thrones*, *The Affair*, and *This Is Us*.

This ideal of marriage as happy conversation constitutes, Cavell says, a 'yes' to marriage that reverses the 'no' of tragedy (as well as the comic 'no' of farces). This 'yes', which is itself a reiteration of an initial episode, is also acceptance of repetition, of the return of days and nights, of the ordinary. It is the culmination of what Cavell calls 'diurnalization', and which we may also refer to as the 'domestication' of scepticism by the ordinary. This work of re-invigorating and familiarizing the ordinary is steadfastly continued by TV series, including fantasy series, for realism has to do not with conformity to the real (a metaphysical question that some series tackle extremely well), but rather with acknowledging it, with the fact of belonging to it and being able to transform it.

Cavell's project for ordinary language realism meant defining the ordinary world on the basis of what we say and mean, and what matters for us. This is summed up in his allusion to Socrates in *Must We Mean What We Say?*: knowing what one means and meaning what one says is the method for knowing the world, or at any rate the ordinary world:

> What they had not realized was what they were saying, or, what they were really saying, and so had not known what they meant. To this extent, they had not known themselves, and not known the world. I mean, of course, the ordinary world. That may not be all there is, but it is important enough: morality is in that world, and so are force and love; so is art and a part of knowledge (the part which is about that world); and so is religion (wherever God is).[38]

We can find in this evocation of the ordinary world, the world of things that matter, a resource for defining ordinary realism, which is limited, so to speak, to the world that matters to us—even if that is not 'all there is'. It is this ordinary world that cinema represents and makes visible. It is within this ordinary world that the characters of TV series evolve. What interests me here is the mode of existence of these characters—not as fictional entities who pose an ontological question, but as beings who matter to us.

For Cavell, realism is defined on the basis of our experience of films; their capacity to elucidate the self through language. True realism is realism of the ordinary. Cavell's ambition is to demonstrate, through both ordinary language and the ontology of cinema, what he calls 'the internality of words and world to one another'.[39] Cavell revolutionized the philosophical approach to cinema and realism itself. In this respect, his work on film is entirely coherent with his work on ordinary language philosophy. *The World Viewed* is an ontological version of his analysis of the stakes of ordinary language philosophy and serves to demonstrate the latter's realism. In 'What Becomes of Things on Film', Cavell specifies that the central aim of his work is to redefine realism not just in film, but *through* film. Film's realism lies not in its representation of reality, but rather in the fact that it is part of our ordinary lives; that the reality of the cinematic experience is integrated in our lives.

Cavell notes that when *The World Viewed* was published in 1971, it was criticized for being 'realist', whereas his goal had been to question whether the various philosophical versions of realism could ever answer the question of the relationship between film and the things of the world, or the question of what becomes of things on screen. What characterizes the experience of cinema is that it is simultaneously mysterious and ordinary—ordinary because nothing is more easily shared and obvious as the fact of going to see movies, and movies provide the material for many of our ordinary conversations. Yet it is also mysterious, because films resemble nothing else and, even now, with the possibility of repeated viewings thanks to video and digital formats, they are evanescent:

> We need always to be returning to the fact of how mysterious these objects called movies are, unlike anything else on earth. They have the evanescence of performances and the permanence of recordings, but they are not recordings (because there is nothing independent of them to which they owe fidelity); and they are not performances (because they are perfectly repeatable).
>
> If what I might call the historical evanescence of film will be overcome ... this should serve to steady our awareness of the natural evanescence of film, the fact that its events exist only in motion, in passing.[40]

There is a proximity here between the experience of film and what constitutes the ordinariness of experience: its evanescence and remanence. This curious harmony is what defines our relationship to the characters on TV series, who are part of our experience. They remain a part of us long after the series has ended. This phenomenon shows us how it is possible to learn from the experience of film, how one can be educated by it, and how, through the experience of it, its objects and characters, one can 'be interested in one's own experience'.[41] Films are part of our experience and 'the difficulty of assessing them is the same as the difficulty of assessing everyday experience'.[42]

For Cavell, to talk about film is not to philosophize with film; rather, it is to find, within philosophy, a way of satisfying the appetite for reality that is born in the cinema. Both Cavell's work on film and his work on ordinary language philosophy make it possible to explore what realism is and to redefine it. Ordinary realism is neither a theory, nor a philosophical argument, nor a metaphysical or ontological position, but rather an exploration of the real. It is not a matter of reaching the real, but of experiencing it; not of proving its existence, but of accepting that one is part of it.[43] In this sense, although Cavell was hardly seduced by pragmatism (from which he always sought to differentiate his work), he is nevertheless a descendant of Dewey and his theory of inquiry. For Cavell, as for Austin, an interest in ordinary language is an interest in the real: 'The philosophy of ordinary language is not about language, anyway not in any sense in which it is not also about the world. Ordinary language philosophy is about whatever ordinary language is about.'[44]

Austin's method allows us to understand a bit more about the nature of our experience of film and of series. Examining ordinary language 'sharpens' our perception of phenomena,[45] and it is this sharpened visual and auditory perception that Cavell was searching for as early as *Must We Mean What We Say?*; for him, the goal of ordinary language philosophy is, as he says in *Pursuits of Happiness*, the 'internality of words and world to one another'.[46] This internality cannot be demonstrated or posited by a 'realist' argument, but can only be shown, as in Austin, through examining our usages and paying attention to the differences language traces:

> When we examine what we should say when, what words we should use in what situations, we are looking again not merely at words (or 'meanings', whatever they may be) but also at the realities we use the words to talk about: we are using a sharpened awareness of words to sharpen our perception of, though not as the final arbiter of, the phenomena.[47]

Cavell writes of 'the appearance and significance of just those objects and people that are in fact to be found in the succession of films, or passages of films, that matter to us'.[48] It is then a question of determining the nature of these appearances and this significance, of this mattering. It is not that cinema gives us a certain perception of our world; rather, it removes us from that world. The particularity of our experience of cinema is that it confronts us with successive projections of the world, a world from which we are necessarily absent. Bourdieu uses the example of *It's a Wonderful Life*, in which the hero is confronted with a world identical in every way to the real world except that in it he does not exist. The moral significance of the movie lies in the sceptical moment when the hero sees a nightmare world from which his (positive) action is absent. He accepts and reintegrates into the world as a result of this experience. Our experience of cinema puts us before a reality in which we do not exist and which no longer exists, but, through this very experience, through the mechanical nature of the projection of the world, we are able to overcome scepticism by living it out: 'Objects on film are always already displaced, *trouvé* (i.e … we as viewers are always already displaced before them).'[49] To be realistic is to accept that things, moments, and people are inscribed in us. To understand what it means to be realistic, one must understand this kind of moral realism. Attention here means a capacity to see details, expressive gestures, even if one does not necessarily have a clear, distinct, or exhaustive view—it is an attention to importance, to what matters in the expressions and styles of others. As Cora Diamond notes, this is what makes for and expresses the moral differences between people: '[To] recognize gestures, manners, habits, turns of speech, turns of thought, styles of face as morally expressive—of an individual or of a people. The intelligent description of such things is part of the intelligent, the sharp-eyed, description of life, of what matters, makes differences, in human lives.'[50]

It is not enough to propose, as Cavell does, that the ontology of film should be defined in terms of importance—for what constitutes the importance of a movie or a moment in a movie? This importance lies in the sharpened perception of characters' ways of being and the ways in which they are woven into our everyday life, integrated into our ordinary existence. The moral expressivity of actors is inseparable from that of the characters they have played:

> Actors in theaters play roles, which might be conceived akin to playing a position in a game. Things are different with film, where with an exemplary performance 'a star is *born*' (*The World Viewed*, 28, emphasis added). Like theater, acting in film is a human activity, saturated by meaning; unlike theater, however, introduced on and through the screen is not a role—to be repeated by others—but instead a distinct individual whose individuality depends *as much* on the unique and expressive physiognomy of the actor or actress in question as it does on the lines fed to him or her.[51]

Just as movies are inscribed within genres, and just as recognizing genres is a form of competence, the roles that movie and TV actors play do not fall into pre-existing categories, but rather are types constituted by 'family resemblance' through the performance of the actor. As Cavell notes, 'On film the type is not primarily the character but primarily the actor.'[52] Similarly, for Shuster, 'Stars are born when novel expressions are born on screen, and actors, with their unique physiognomies and physicalities, are essential to that birth.'[53] The various remakes of the movie *A Star is Born* have each, in their own way, captured the moment when star quality 'bursts onto the screen'—that is, it is shown and becomes perceptible, real to us. Even Bradley Cooper's contestable version (2018) includes one of the most beautiful scenes of the revelation of a human vocal texture when Ally (Lady Gaga) takes the microphone for the first time on stage and makes her voice heard, becoming a star.

In classic cinema, we observe the emergence of a specific kind of object: the moral type comprising the various roles an actor has played. The resulting moral texture is the material of the moral realism that series allow us to define. Thus we can analyse the impact that actors and characters have had on our lives, becoming part of us and mattering to us just like the real people we are close to. In this respect, the effects that, for example, an actor's physical transformations over the course of a series have on our attachments to them are more relevant and useful for thinking about realism than contemporary cinema's various attempts at creating non-existent worlds or multiple levels of reality. Such attempts—movies such as *Blade Runner 2049* (Villeneuve,

2017), *The Matrix* (The Wachowskis, 1999–2021), *The Truman Show* (Peter Weir, 1998), *The Majestic* (Frank Darabont, 2001), *Inception* (Christopher Nolan, 2010), and so on—are useful, but ultimately unconvincing.

As Wittgenstein suggests, moral philosophy must shift its field of study from the examination of general concepts to that of particular visions, what Iris Murdoch called the 'configurations' of individuals' thought, which 'show continually in their reactions and conversation. These things, which may be overtly and comprehensibly displayed or inwardly elaborated and guessed at, constitute what, making different points in the two metaphors, one may call the texture of a man's being or the nature of his personal vision.'[54] It is in someone's use of language (their choice of expressions, style of speech, involvement in the exchange) that their moral vision is seen or developed. For Murdoch, this moral vision is not a theoretical or epistemic point of view but rather a texture of being (and texture can be visual, auditory, or tactile). Paying attention to texture makes it possible to see what is important, as well as that which comprises and expresses the differences between individuals. Attention to the texture of characters over time educates us, as does attention to the moral consistency of others—and attention to others *tout court*.

These differences are what we must pay attention to in order to produce 'the intelligent, the sharp-eyed, description of life, of what matters, makes differences in human lives' that Diamond speaks of.[55] This human life corresponds to a Wittgensteinian form of life, which also defines a texture of the real and of words: the sensitivity of our words and statements to their usages. Thus, texture designates an unstable reality, one that cannot be nailed down by determinate concepts or objects, but rather entails the recognition of human gestures and styles. This is the *real* of TV series ('the ordinary world').

From an ethical point of view, the human form of life, a central theme in Wittgenstein's work,[56] as well as in other movements of contemporary thought (critical theory, for example), is suffused with perception and attention to moral textures and motifs, to ways of being. These motifs are 'morally expressive' and constitute elements of the grammar of ethical individuation. Thus, it is not a matter of viewing objects through the lens of morality or values, but rather of paying attention to moral expression, which is only possible and visible against the backdrop of the human form of life. For philosophers such as Diamond and Nussbaum, literature is an ideal site for moral perception because it creates a background against which important differences appear, and for Cavell the same is true of cinema. The same can also be said of the rich material provided by TV series: today, series are the most relevant frameworks for moral education and attention—and are no doubt more democratic than novels.

Like our attachment to movie characters, our attachment to the TV characters who affect us and with whom we concern ourselves (e.g., looking them up online or editing Wikipedia pages about them) is based on a physical reality that has been recorded. Yet in the case of the latter, the recording occurs over a timespan of years, which is rarely the case in cinema, apart from a few wonderful experiments such as *Boyhood* (Richard Linklater, 2014), or, more trivially, movie franchises and series. The continued presence of a TV series character over the long term goes hand in hand with a set of physical changes: growing up and aging (the whole group on *Friends*, Jack on *24*, Rick on *The Walking Dead*, Walter and Skyler White in *Breaking Bad*, and Arya on *Game of Thrones*, or changes in hairstyle and weight (Betty Draper on *Mad Men*, Angel on *Buffy* and *Angel*). These elements shed light on the ontology of what matters (characters are real because they matter to us, we care about them) and show the pressure of reality: we become attached to actors, to physical people, who transform over time and whose changes attach us to them and to their characters indistinguishably—whence the pleasure of seeing them again on a different series. I am thinking here of examples such as Alyson Hannigan (from *Buffy* to *How I Met Your Mother*), Mary Louise Parker (from *The West Wing* to *Weeds* and *Blacklist*), Edie Falco (from *Oz* to *The Sopranos* and *Nurse Jackie*) and of course Bryan Cranston from *Malcolm in the Middle* to *Breaking Bad* and *Your Honor*—not to mention surprising come-backs such as that of Henry Winkler on *Barry* (2018), Jeff Bridges in *The Old Man* (2022) or the reappearance of the characters from *Twin Peaks* twenty-six years later on *Twin Peaks: The Return*, more or less ravaged by the passing of time. It is on these occasions that we realize that they have become part of us; that they have remained buried within us like some strange hidden family that continues to age along with us.

Thus, we understand that TV series touch on the nature of experience itself, which is defined by our capacity for attention and attachment. It is indeed a matter of care—to use Murdoch's expression, of 'unsentimental, detached, unselfish, objective attention'.[57] The fact that these characters do not actually live with us, that they come from a world in which we do not exist, but which we explore with them, is, paradoxically, a reality effect (*effet de réel*): 'Film's presenting of the world by absenting us from it appears as confirmation of something already true of our stage of existence. Its displacement of the world confirms, even explains, our prior estrangement from it. The "sense of reality" provided on film is the sense of *that* reality, one from which we already sense a distance.'[58]

The kind of attention I have been describing is a capacity to see details and expressive gestures, even without a clear or complete view. It is attention to importance, to what matters, in others' expressions and styles; to what accounts for and expresses the differences between individuals; to how each person relates to their experience. To pay attention to the ordinary is thus to perceive moral textures or motifs. One meaning of importance is thus the ability to know what matters, what is important to you. As I have mentioned, it is care for the characters on TV series that constitutes the most relevant ethical method here. These characters are so rooted in our lives, so morally guided and clear in their moral expressions, that they are 'entrusted' to us, and remain so for life. Care here is understood as attention to the particularities of the real and to the importance of a given moment: the reality of the presence of fictional characters in ordinary life (the problem is no longer ontological, but rather moral); the production of a line of expression.

The viewer's connection to characters leads to sharing their knowledge and entering into their professional worlds; acquiring objective knowledge about hospitals, the police, the justice system, politics, prisons, prostitution, intelligence services, office work, and so on. We enrich our experience by visiting these characters on a regular basis over the long term. Such experience may be acquired at the movies or in literature, but in series, it is multiplied over time, and its temporality matches the real time of learning. Furthermore, this experience allows the viewer to refine their judgement: to practise, in a sense; to become better at using their judgement and at trusting their experience.

Series are a way of giving public expression to a moral experience that is most often experienced within the private sphere. What, precisely, does this experience consist of? Care is not just a central topic in series; series are also ways of arousing care (by awakening affectivity, and by showing us characters who move us). We can see this with *ER*, both in its moving depictions of situations involving one-off characters, but also in the real attachment created by the repeated contact with its regular cast of characters. Some of the show's most intense moments are those in which a character is ill or dies (Jeanie Boulet, Mark Greene). These extreme moments make clear the kind of attachments we develop to fictional characters, which can only be understood in terms of care.

Thus, we cannot discuss the importance of series and their specific realism without describing the connections that we form to TV characters over the course of episodes. As Thibaut de Saint Maurice has noted,[59] our connection to series is forged precisely through characters—without characters, there can be no series. It is they, more than directors or screenwriters, and even more than the plot or aesthetic of a series, that determine whether we like a show and want to continue watching it. From the beginning, series have given characters consistency: they remain true to themselves from episode to episode and from season to season. And part of the pleasure and affection we feel comes from finding characters back in their places, reuniting with them after the break between seasons. But characters can also be unstable; they change and vary as the show or the plot develop—sometimes radically, examples being Jimmy McNulty in season 5 of *The Wire*, Rick again on *The Walking Dead*, and Piper Chapman on *Orange Is the New Black*—but sometimes imperceptibly, like the moral character of Saul Goodman during the 6 seasons of *Better Call Saul*.

Characters define the realism of series—like real people, characters are at once the same and other, familiar and strange. Attachment is made possible by regularity and by contact over the long term, and without this series' characters could not exist. (It is not clear whether the same attachment occurs with miniseries, which have proliferated of late; there, the attachment may be closer to the kind we form to movie characters, which obviously continues to represent a major fact of our collective experience.)

Family or families are at the core of *Game of Thrones*, obviously, and of *House of the Dragon*, one of the most popular recent shows, which took over from the mythical series, although the action is set two hundred years earlier, at the origin of one of the most important families of the saga. *House of the Dragon* has many differences from its "parent" series - including, for the time being, a relative absence of major geopolitical struggles and military engagements. Most of the politics here are played out in a war of succession, which is why this series has been compared to Jesse Armstrong's magnificent work *Succession*, which portrays the rivalry of the children of a media mogul. We find in this first season of *House of the Dragon* a similar plot with the multiple betrayals, hatreds and reversals of alliances that agitate a quasi-nuclear family revolving around the father, Viserys (Paddy Considine, in a striking role), whose announced demise creates an interminable expectation over the course of the episodes; like that of another father, the one in *This Is Us* (who dies endlessly). This theme of succession is at the same time that of generation, which materializes in *House of the Dragon* in the most concrete way, by the multiplication of the scenes of childbirth.

Since the 1980s, we have seen a shift away from series based on a sole, usually male, and often titular character—*Columbo, MacGyver, Dexter, House*—and toward series that do away with the notion of a main character by focusing on a group of characters (e.g., *ER, Friends, Desperate Housewives, Game of Thrones*). In between, there was a doubling of the main character, giving rise to shows about duos—*Starsky and Hutch, Moonlighting, Miami Vice*, and, in our century, the first season of *True Detective*, thereby confirming the show's retro side. The traditional distinction between main characters and secondary characters—and thus between primary and secondary roles—has been effaced, which is logical, since for a long time these secondary roles have been essential to the moral and realistic texture of films and series. The distinction can also evolve over the course of a series. In the first season of *Game of Thrones*, for example, Tyrion Lannister was a secondary character, but he became a main character in the second season—something exceptional for someone of his size. Similarly, the character of McNulty is almost entirely absent from season four of *The Wire* (not that we miss him too much). Curiously enough, a character played by the same actor, Dominic West, is gradually effaced over the course of the fourth season of *The Affair* as well. That unique series stands out for the way in which it detaches from its main plot: the 'affair' of the title, from which we quickly move on and which is initially recounted only from the point of view of its two main characters, Noah and Alison. The show then shifts focus and foregrounds characters who were harmed and embittered as a result of the affair: the former spouses of the romantic heroes. Gradually, Helen, the abandoned wife who was humiliated in the first season, becomes the centre of the show. Her ironic smile in the last shot of the fourth season places her at the heart of the story and of the moral understanding of what happens in it.

Not all recent series feature group heroes, but they do all call into question the secondary nature of secondary characters. This is not surprising, for what is a supporting role but one played by an actor who carries the series, or who manages to make a lasting impression in a brief or unobtrusive appearance? This emphasis on the secondary is made possible in particular by the time that creators have to bring each character to life, sometimes even dedicating an entire episode to them, as *Buffy* did, and as *The Walking Dead* does fairly often (sometimes to excess, it must be said).

Between the elements that make up a collective hero we always find what Wittgenstein called 'family resemblances'. And this is not by chance. As de Saint Maurice and Shuster have shown, the family is the base structure of series, just as the heterosexual couple is the base structure of comedies of remarriage and many other Hollywood genres. The characters on series are defined by the fact that, through the logic of repetition, they develop family-like relationships, and thus they acquire family resemblances. The creation of such 'family resemblances' between characters facilitates the viewer's integration into the group or universe of the series. The greatness of the series *This Is Us* lies in how it transfers the question of the creation of family bonds onto a real family (the complexity of the show's composition and plot allows for it). Of course, it is not the only series to feature a family as a character—see *Six Feet Under* and the excellent and fun *Modern Family*. But *This is Us* is the only one that builds the family's bonds across its episodes and narrative arc, overcoming scepticism, against all ruptures, losses, and stereotypes. The beauty of the first episode is to reunite the apparently broken family, from the striking conclusion of the episode with the story of the birth of the three children and the constitution of the family that will then weave and break and rebuild its links. *This is Us* is probably the last great classic series in this sense, radicalizing and exhausting the subject of the majority of the series. The series leading us to integrate and adopt, like the Pearson family, all sorts of new members in our imaginary family, by concentric circles—up to missing brothers, new spouses of ex-spouses or friends of biological parents. A definition of inclusiveness.

Over the past few years, we have left behind (or have been left by), among other extraordinary shows, *The Affair, Homeland, The Bureau, Ozark, Better Call Saul*, and *This Is Us*. This experience is always accompanied by sadness, and leaves us wondering what would happen to our favourite heroes if we could continue our journey together. The difficulty of parting from series characters is a remarkable phenomenon that reveals the strong attachment we develop towards characters we see on a regular basis: characters, plural, because nowadays there are hardly any series with just one hero. Long narrative arcs allow for the recurrence of secondary characters. This recurrence, over the run of a series, weakens the hierarchy between main and secondary characters. Thus, it is difficult to speak of a series character in the singular, given that series' narratives are inextricably intertwined with the collective destiny of their heroes. Instead, it is more productive to speak of an ensemble, a cast of characters.

The causes of our attachment to characters or to the actors who play them are complex and not just a matter of identification, or even of complicity or admiration, and they change over the duration of the show. In some series, the very status of characters can change: in *Orange is the New Black*, a 'secondary' character such as Poussey takes centre stage in numerous episodes. There are several shows that challenge our sense of attachment by killing off characters who have been essential to the narrative: this is, of course, the case in *Game of Thrones* and *The Walking Dead*. *Ozark*, for example, shows us our attachment to Ruth Langmore (the brilliant Julia Garner), at first not part of the central "family" cast, by making us realize the show is simply over when she dies. *Better Call Saul* demonstrates the strategic place of Saul Goodman even in *Breaking Bad*, where he seemed a secondary, even funny character—as if giving an a posteriori understanding of a further narrative. Thus, our attachment to a series cannot anymore be reduced solely to the experience of attachment to a single character. Some secondary characters will come to haunt us all our lives, like Wallace and Snoop from *The Wire*, Jane from *Breaking Bad*, Chuck McGill in *Better Call Saul*; or become quintessential to a series. It is hard to imagine that Jesse Pinkman was supposed to die at the end of the first season of *Breaking Bad*.

Ensemble series with numerous characters such as *Games of Thrones*, *The Walking Dead*, or the excellent French show *Engrenages (Spiral* for English-language markets*)* represent their characters as members of the same family. Whether they are part of an actual family or not, the relationships between these people become increasingly familiar to us. There is a familialization of the series' cast. This familiarity of series characters, in the double sense of what is familiar/close to us and what constitutes a family for us, helps describe the possibility of a collective bond—and also establishes the central element of long-running series: the family. This is at the heart of recent series, replacing the individual or the couple, which were the central subjects of classic cinema (Westerns, crime thrillers, romantic comedies, etc.). It was the subject of *The Sopranos*, *Six Feet Under*, *Breaking Bad*, *The Americans*, *Modern Family*, and of course *Game of Thrones*; it is even more prominently the main subject of *Succession*, *Ozark*, and *This Is Us*—even if these families are twisted, blended, or might appear atypical. It is this ensemble or familial character that allows for an attachment to even unsympathetic or ambivalent characters, as in *Ozark*.

The major series thus operate through familialization by establishing associations between the characters over the years; and even when we are not dealing with a family at the start, we become a part of one at the end. *Mad Men* and *The Bureau* are interesting illustrations of this, when families are formed from professional groups. By the very logic of their long-term association, the characters in the series are led to develop family-type relationships, and to integrate us into them. It is because of this aspect of series that we find it difficult to extricate ourselves from the characters.

This is the case with the iconic family series *Ozark*—a 'white trash' series that is an unexpected choice for a 'prestige' Netflix show. The series starts with the culture shock of a city-dwelling family, the Byrdes, who move to Missouri under duress to revive a money-laundering operation for a powerful Mexican cartel. Long underrated, *Ozark* is one of Netflix's best productions; it is an example of a family series that roots itself in a family structure, while also creating an extended family beyond the nuclear Byrde family. It brings all its characters together in a 'type', a grey area between good and evil—the Byrdes, Marty and Wendy, increasingly slide towards the latter in the later seasons. The temporality of the series makes their slow moral degradation even more impactful—and this is a great asset of family series (as in *Game of Thrones* and *The Americans*)—through the moral and physical evolution of the children. This family solidarity becomes complete in the last seconds of the series (but no spoilers).

It is also only in a long-running series that we could discover a female character as demented and deviant as Darlene Snell or a figure as hypocritical and fascinating as Wendy Byrde, Laura Linney's great role. Ruth Langmore, a character whose strength and vulnerable intelligence actually carry the series through to the final tragedy, must also be added to *Ozark*'s set of exceptional, tough, and compelling female characters who give the series its moral radicalism.

Ozark has been compared to *Succession* on the basis of the moral transgressions committed by its unlikable or, in the case of the latter, downright vile, characters. *Ozark*'s characters are indeed morally dubious and disturbing—yet not to the point of turning attachment into hatred. They remain ordinary people, sometimes likable, always capable of disappointing us, and also of reassuring us. The final season offers several points of revelation. Leaving the series is like being torn away from a family that is twisted but very much our own.

The family genre is at the heart of the beautiful series *Better Things*, whose heroine is Sam Fox, an LA actress who chases castings and multiplies small, seedy roles while raising her three daughters alone. *Better Things* is not a journey of self-exploration or transformation, but consistently asserts an ordinary point of view, presenting in first person the daily life of a totally disillusioned 50-year-old woman. Sam, at the end of the series, achieves a form of separation from her family herself, much like *The Americans*, which sees parents abandoned by their children. But the tragic melancholy of *The Americans* gives way in *Better Things* to a perfectionist optimism, where leaving the family or at least taking distance creates new possibilities for self-development.

Yet the most striking recent event in this respect has been the conclusion of the beautiful series *This Is Us*, a quintessential family series whose characters have become deeply embedded in our experience, in large part thanks to outstanding acting performances, including the extraordinary Sterling K. Brown (Randall), that carry the series to its end.

The series is built entirely around the story of a family over three generations. The first two seasons are steeped in the anxious anticipation of the untimely death of the dynasty's patriarch Jack Pearson, which is hinted at in the early episodes. As a point of symmetry, the last two seasons focus on the more predictable death of the matriarch, Rebecca. This loops back to the founding episode of the series, that of the birth of the 'Big Three'. The pilot, which blended the present and the past—Kate's, Kevin's, and Randall's 36th birthday and the day they were born—displayed the series' method of looping back to past events in order to allow us to understand them in a variety of new ways. The pilot gradually and skilfully revealed the bond between these three very different people—a black man, a white woman, and a white man—by showing the founding events of the series, Rebecca's difficult delivery of triplets with the birth of two twins, Kate and Kevin, and the tragedy of the third baby's death, as well as the Pearson couple's adoption of an abandoned African-American baby on the same day. The following seasons tell the story of the difficulties of the adult lives, but also of the childhoods, of the Big Three, the premature death of their father, Jack, his youth, that of his brother Nick, and of William, Randall's biological father. The narrative, which moves back and forth between different periods in the characters' lives, allows—as in any long-running series—not just the characters, but also their relationships, to deepen.

Within the elements of this collective hero family, we find again what Wittgenstein calls family resemblances. The greatness of *This Is Us* lies in the fact that it projects the idea of bonding onto a real family, which is made possible by the complexity of its composition and history. The beauty of the first episode is that it brings together a seemingly broken family, while the whole series proceeds to make a family out of the various traumatic events that the protagonists have experienced. Of course, this is not the only show to use a family as a character, but *This is Us* is the only one today that builds familial links through all its episodes and the narrative of the show.

In this sense, *This is Us* may be the last great classic series, simultaneously radicalizing and exhausting the subject matter of the majority of twenty-first-century series. It is the series that led us to integrate and adopt, like the Pearson family, all sorts of new members into our imaginary family, in concentric circles—right down to the missing brother, the new spouses of the ex-spouses, friends of the biological parents, and more: the definition of inclusiveness.

This Is Us has thus become more political over its run, presenting the multigenerational fate of a white, middle-class family that adopted a black child in the 1980s. Rebecca Pearson, at the beginning of the second season, recalls the moment in the first episode of the series when, in the maternity ward, having lost one of her triplets, she is persuaded by Jack, her husband, to adopt an abandoned black baby, Randall: *'This stranger became my child and this child became my life.'* *This Is Us* affirms that the United States is mixed and multiple, in its history and its present, in this *us* that embodies *US(A)* beyond the Pearsons, and beyond the USA (the French adaptation, *Je te promets*, is remarkable and just as politically bold).

The pedagogy of the show goes even further, since in the fifth, post-COVID-19 season, Randall sees the news of George Floyd's death on his phone, which deeply upsets him. From that point forward, *This Is Us* confronts head-on the question of race through a powerful return to the trajectory of Randall's life, a black child raised in a white, loving, 'color-blind' family. As viewers, we come to realize that what we saw from the beginning as a beautiful story of integration was *also* a painful story of denial. This is the lesson of *This Is Us*—it teaches us not by making us love this story and these characters any less, but by making us understand some (not necessarily pleasant) things about ourselves. Throughout the series, the characters' neuroses and imperfections endear them to us, because they create the flaws and vulnerabilities where our care can be elicited.

The finale, written by the show's creator Dan Fogelman and simply titled 'Us', could have been an unending fest of emotion and tears. Instead, it is strikingly short for a finale, humbly returning us to the ordinary life of a nondescript, lazy Sunday in the Pearson family, when the little ones were 10 years old. Opening with Jake and Rebecca waking up and going through a thousand little things of family life, this 106th episode reveals what has historically been the show's strength: highlighting the little moments that crystallize the value of a family and make up the salt of life (to use Françoise Héritier's phrase and the title of her wonderful book). In its final moments, *This Is Us* finds itself by the side of Jack and Randall, two exceptional characters whom the series has been able to create from totally new family ties. It should not be forgotten that this beautiful series was aired on a traditional television network, NBC, using a model that was thought to be outdated: one that makes us wait impatiently for what will happen next week, with new episodes and the return of the seasons. Are these long-running series, which carry us with them for five or more years and become part of our experience and the temporality of our lives, a disappearing format? We have now entered a different temporality, that of miniseries formatted for a long weekend, to be viewed on laptops and smartphones. These are often excellent, but their incursions into our personal history, and no doubt their position within the history of series, are, with a few brilliant exceptions, more limited.

Notes

1   Cavell, 'The Fact of Television', p. 77.
2   Ibid., p. 85 (emphasis added).
3   Cavell, *The World Viewed*, p. 48.
4   Cavell, 'The Fact of Television', p. 85 (emphasis added).
5   Ibid., pp. 78–79.
6   Ibid., p. 78.
7   First published in *Artspace*, May–June 1988; reprinted in *Cavell on Film*, pp. 167–74.
8   Rothman, 'Introduction', *Cavell on Film*, p. xxiv.
9   Ibid.
10   Cavell, *Pursuits*, 41.
11   Cavell, 'The Fact of Television', p. 77.

12 See Laugier, *Why We Need Ordinary Language Philosophy*.

13 Cavell, 'What Becomes of Things on Film?' in *Themes*, p. 183.

14 Laugier, *Éthique, littérature, vie humaine*; Cora Diamond, *L'importance d'être humain* (Paris: PUF, 2011).

15 Cavell, 'The Good of Film', in *Cavell on Film*, p. 336.

16 Cavell, *The World Viewed*, p. 12.

17 Stanley Cavell, *Must We Mean What We Say?* (Cambridge: Cambridge University Press, 1969); Laugier, *Wittgenstein*.

18 Cavell, *The World Viewed*, p. 154.

19 Rosalind E. Krauss, 'Rosalind Krauss on Dark Glasses and Bifocals', *Artforum* 12, no. 9 (May 1974): 59–62, https://www.artforum.com/print/197405/dark-glasses-and-bifocals-37376. See Clémot, *Cinéthique*.

20 Cavell, 'More of the World Viewed', in *The World Viewed*, pp. 162–230.

21 Ogien and Laugier, *Le principe démocratie*, chapter 5.

22 Ferrarese and Laugier, *Formes de vie*, p. 7.

23 Bourdieu, in Cerisuelo and Laugier, *Stanley Cavell: Cinéma et philosophie*, p. 46 [translated from the French original].

24 Cavell, *Pursuits*, p. 41.

25 Stanley Cavell, *The Senses of Walden*, expanded edition (Chicago: University of Chicago Press, 1992).

26 Emerson, 'The American Scholar', in Ralph Waldo Emerson, *The Essential Writings of Ralph Waldo Emerson*, edited by Brooks Atkinson (New York: Modern Library, 2000), p. 57.

27 Wittgenstein, *Philosophical Investigations*, §116.

28 Sandra Laugier, 'The Ordinary, Romanticism, and Democracy' *MLN*, Vol. 130, No. 5, Comparative Literature Issue: Practices of the Ordinary (December 2015), pp. 1040–1054. https://www.jstor.org/stable/43932910

29 See Shuster, *New Television*.

30 Stanley Cavell, *In Quest of the Ordinary: Lines of Skepticism and Romanticism* (Chicago: University of Chicago Press, 1988), p. 4.

31 Cavell, *Pursuits*, p. 8.

32 Ibid., pp. 8, 9.

33 John Dewey, *Art as Experience* (New York: Perigee, 1980), p. 294.

34 Cavell, 'The Good of Film', in *Cavell on Film*, p. 340.

35 Cavell, *Claim of Reason*, p. 125.

36 Northrop Frye, *Anatomy of Criticism* (Princeton, NJ: Princeton University Press, 2020), pp. 43–44.

37 Cavell, *Contesting Tears* (emphasis added for 'conversation', in the original for 'fact').

38 Cavell, *Must We Mean What We Say?*, p. 40.

39 Cavell, *Pursuits*, p. 204.

40 Cavell, 'The Thought of Movies', in *Cavell on Film*, p. 94.

41 Cavell, *Pursuits*, p. 41.

42 Ibid.

43 See Sandra Laugier, *Why We Need Ordinary Language Philosophy*, translated by Daniela Ginsburg (Chicago: University of Chicago Press, 2013), where I defend this argument.

44 Cavell, *Must We Mean*, p. 95.

45 J.L. Austin, *Philosophical Papers*, second edition (Oxford: Clarendon Press, 1970), p. 182.

46 Cavell, *Pursuits*, p. 204.

47 Austin, *Philosophical Papers*, p. 182.

48 Cavell, 'What Becomes', in *Themes*, p. 183.

49 Ibid.

50 Diamond, *The Realistic Spirit*, p. 375.

51 Shuster, *New Television*, p. 50.

52 Cavell, *The World Viewed*, p. 174.

53 Shuster, *New Television*, p. 51.

54 Iris Murdoch, 'Vision and Choice in Morality', in *Existentialists and Mystics: Writings on Philosophy and Literature*, edited by Iris Murdoch and Peter J. Conradi (London: Chatto & Windus, 1997), p. 82.

55 Diamond, *The Realistic Spirit*, p. 375.

56 See Ferrarse and Laugier, *Formes de vie*.

57 Iris Murdoch, 'On "God" and "Good"', in *Existentialists and Mystics*, p. 353.

58 Cavell, 'More of The World Viewed', in *The World Viewed*, p. 226.

59 Thibaut de Saint Maurice, 'Portrait du sériephile en philosophe', in *Le pouvoir des liens faibles*, edited by Alexandre Gefen and Sandra Laugier (Paris: CNRS, 2020).

Caring for, By, and With TV Series

For Wittgenstein, concepts are constructed through the family resemblances between different usages of signs; similarly, attachment to characters is created through the family resemblances between them. In his fascinating work *La Sériephilie, sociologie d'un attachement culturel*, Hervé Glévarec discovers over the course of interviews with high school students that their interest in characters comes from the fact that we will find out what happens in their lives.

> Romain, 23 years old: 'I don't think it's necessary to identify with one character, because really we appreciate them all. We appreciate them all and maybe because each character has different characteristics and the whole forms a character we would really like maybe, I don't know. But no, I don't think it's necessary to identify with one.'[1]

Indeed, identification is no longer the only way of thinking about attachment, since, beginning in the 1990s, certain emblematic characters have provoked strong attachments without any (conscious) identification: Andy Sipowicz, Don Draper, Dexter, Walter White, Jesse Pinkman, Hannah Horvath, Jimmy McNulty, Jimmy McGill/Saul Goodman, Michael Ehrmantraut, Omar, Malotru, Eve and Villanelle, or Dougie on *Twin Peaks*.

I become attached to a character because they interest me; they teach me how to understand what interests me, what matters to me, and, as Cavell recommended to his students, how to be interesting. I become attached because the character allows me to explore my life, and my own moral choices—because their life allows me to question and investigate my own. One important aspect of the moral education that serves as my guiding thread throughout this work comes from the conversation that the viewer has with their own moral conceptions, a conversation that draws on the ordinary, intense moral life of anyone who resonates with a series.

This gives rise to the curious phenomenon of a joint attachment to several characters at once, and to their relationships within a series. And it gives rise to attachment to characters who are quite different from us. All these characters, who often come from professional milieus to which we have little, if any, access—the police service, medicine, prisons (all Foucauldian themes)—allow us to satisfy a certain curiosity about or fascination with these worlds. If the couple (or love) is the primary narrative pivotal point in film, in series, as we have said, the family is central—but so is work. *ER, Six Feet Under, The West Wing, Mad Men, Baron Noir, The Bureau* introduce us not only to mysterious professional worlds, but also show us relations between colleagues, micro-conflicts within the hierarchy, and the chain of command (higher-ups not doing their jobs, etc.). What is interesting is that all these series foreground both work and care (or the work of care in the case of medical or post-mortem legal series).

It is worth pausing and asking why *Mad Men*, a series about advertising (a field that is often the object of intellectuals' contempt), met with such success among an elitist audience. By coming into daily contact with the community of advertising executives on *Mad* Men, by sharing in the reality of their work and their form of life, we come to see the beauty of everyday objects and to reflect on what we appreciate in existence; to aestheticize our lives. As they search for slogans, the characters on *Mad Men* are in search of the right word, in Wittgenstein's sense (not the word that would exactly capture a feeling or thought; rather, they seek to express as accurately as possible what matters in a capitalist world in which traditional values are beginning to crumble). The real ethnographic work that series perform allows the viewer to discover not only professional universes but also different cultures and civilizations—from the small Southern towns in *True Blood* and *Justified* to the world of lesbians in southern California in *The L Word* and to farming communities in the third season of *American Crime*. From this point of view, there are still many possible series to be made about little-known worlds, and perhaps anthropology will replace philosophy as the engine of series.

Attachment to series rests not on their ability to duplicate or 'represent' the real, but rather to explore it concretely. Security series such as *The Bureau* are no doubt the most notable in this respect, by giving democratic access to the domain of intelligence services and state secrets that, by definition, are kept out of reach of the ordinary citizen. The first episode of *ER*, where we see Dr Mark Greene's day in all its details, and the first scene of *The Bureau*, in which a new recruit is introduced and is initiated into the practices and rituals of the DGSE, are emblematic of this exploratory dimension. Attachment occurs over the course of repeated, regular contact, something Aurélien, 25 years old, expresses in a touching quote reported by Glevarec: 'I think *Friends* really lives up to its name. It's a group of friends and in spite of everything they are people you would really like to have as friends, because they have their good and bad qualities . . . We feel pain of the characters, we are happy for them, like friends ultimately.'[2] These reflections from an ordinary viewer reveal the true nature of our connection to characters. If they challenge us, it is not because they are 'like us' and we identify with them. It is because with all their particularities, they touch us, they affect us. Because we care about what happens to them, even if it is not our own life.

Or rather, because it *is* our life. Our life in series.

This recalls what Cavell said about the movies that matter to us, whose scenes become entwined with our personal memories. Their characters live within us, and movies 'become further fragments of what happens to me, further cards in the shuffle of my memory'.[3] Proof of this affection can be found everywhere on the Internet: web forums, sites dedicated to discussing a series or a character, detailed Wikipedia pages for even the most minor characters (for instance, from *The Walking Dead*). At stake in this affection is a moral bond. Series make attention into a moral experience.

We are attached to characters because we have become attentive to them. Care is here and in the companion volume *TV-Philosophy in Action* understood as attention to the particularities of the real and to the importance of a certain moment, character, or situation—the reality of the presence of fictional characters in ordinary life. It is not surprising that this form of attachment is mobilized in particular in final scenes—at the moment when we must detach from these characters, at the moment when attachment changes form. This presence of a character within us defines both the ontology and the moral power of series' heroes.[4] This power and this reality last well beyond the duration of a series, either its airing or viewing. Sabine Chalvon ironizes delightfully about the lifespan of what she calls the TSH (TV series hero): 'We might say that the lifespan of the TSH, his or her persistence in our memory, does not last much longer than the life cycle of a series—that is, on average, between 7 and 10 years. So the TSH doesn't live much longer than a dog.'[5] But it is possible that here, for once, she is mistaken. If we consider that the TSH lives within us and that this composite entity, subjectively inscribed within us, lasts as long as the character matters to us, then we may say that the 'great' characters (Buffy, Omar, the Fishers, Don Draper, Dexter, Walter White, Elizabeth Jennings . . .) live for a very long time, even a lifetime.

The duration of series and their recurrence (the regular return of episodes and seasons) allows them to expand time, as the series *24* does, using the device of real time to make one of Agent Jack Bauer's days last as long as a TV season—or, on the contrary, to condense time, such that a season passes in a few minutes, as in the joyful sixteenth episode of *Twin Peaks: The Return*, in which we are finally reunited with our old friend Dale Cooper from the first two seasons. However, we quickly lose him again, and not just because he has an evil twin. The final episode is a veritable descent into hell for anyone attached to Cooper and even to Dougie, his first reincarnation in *Twin Peaks: The Return*. Dale Cooper gradually becomes unrecognizable and is lost. The uncanniness we usually find in Lynch's work is pushed even further here, for we radically lose contact with the most important characters of the series, who have shaped our experience of it. The meaning of 'return' in the title is thus tragically converted: the world that Cooper's return seemed to have restored to us is torn from us again. Frost and Lynch position the television series within the sceptical tradition proposed by Cavell, but they take scepticism one step further: if they give the world back to us, it is only in order to better deprive us of it. The effect of the restoration of the world and its lively intensity (Cooper's joviality and the jubilation of the episode) is to make us even more radically strangers to it.

Thus, the ordinary realism of series passes through characters and our attachment to them, as our feeling of radical loss when a character is taken from us proves. Care, ultimately, is a tool of realism, which is indeed a matter of trust—a matter of knowing how and when to trust your experience, to find the validity specific to the particular. Regaining contact with experience and finding a voice to express it: this is the primary—perfectionist and political—aim of ethics. What remains is to connect our subjective experience to the attention to the particular that is at the heart of care, and to define knowledge through care. This is the moral knowledge that literary, cinematic, and televisual works give us by educating our sensibility and morals at once—whence Nussbaum's wonderful, ambiguous title, 'Love's Knowledge', which refers not to knowledge of some object, love, but rather to the particular knowledge that comes to us through perception refined by attention, the kind of knowledge we gain through TV series.

Ethics is attention to others and to the way in which they (like us) exist within connections. Any ethics of film and series is thus an ethics of care, of concern for others. This is why the twentieth century produced new attention to the real through the experience of cinema, and why the twenty-first century is continuing to change our perception of the real even more, through an even more repeated, ordinary, and domestic experience, that of series. Popular American films of the late twentieth century foregrounded the attention and agency specific to care and the wide diversity of its forms. Here we may mention Lloyd Dobler, the character played by John Cusack in *Say Anything* (an under-recognized film to which Cavell draws our attention). The entire film (and this is even *the* subject of the film) demonstrates Lloyd's capacity to take care of the girl he loves, Diane. In a famous scene at dinner with her parents, when asked about his future career plans, Lloyd responds: 'I don't want to sell anything, buy anything, or process anything'; what he wants to do is take care of Diane: 'What I really want to do with my life—what I want to do for a living—is I want to be with your daughter. I'm good at it.' The entire film (and Cusack's performance) is designed to make us like and respect Lloyd, to notice and appreciate what he does. The theme of care is present in Crowe's other cult film, *Jerry Maguire* (1996), with Renée Zellweger and Tom Cruise, again centred on care. Care is present in a unique way in *Pulp Fiction* in which John Travolta's character, a gangster, has to 'take care' of his boss's girlfriend. The choice of phrase leads to some confusion; his conversation partner asks if by this he means that he has to kill her. Despite this less than promising beginning, he does in fact take care of her, taking her out dancing, winning a dance competition with her, and ultimately saving her life by resuscitating her after a drug overdose.

Care is even more central a theme in TV series, no doubt owing to the way in which they allow a multiplicity of moral positions and voices to exist within the same world. The polyphonic nature of series makes possible a plurality of unique expressions and allows for the depiction of arguments, debates, and misunderstandings—and thus an education in attention. It is this methodology of series—not only their narrativity, but also and above all how they present and construct characters—that makes for their moral relevance and expressiveness. However, this obliges us to revise the status of morality and to see it not in rules and principles of decision-making, but in attention to ordinary behaviour, daily micro-choices, and individuals' styles of expression. The material of TV series allows for contextualization, historicity (regularity, duration), familiarization, and an education of perception (attention to the expressions and gestures of characters we come to know well, but who still have the capacity to totally surprise us). Understanding this requires taking seriously the moral intentions of television producers and screenwriters, and the constraints thus imposed on works of fiction—here again in line with Cavell's reading, which broke with the critical tradition of seeing the intelligence and significance of a film as a by-product of critical reading, and affirmed instead the importance of the fact that films are collectively written, and the role of screenwriters, directors, and actors, in developing the significance and educational value of a film.

Here we may think of the importance of the series *Buffy the Vampire Slayer* and the paradoxical way Buffy embodies care (care for her friends, her mother, her sister—as well as for the world, which she saves on a regular basis). This allows her to be a role model for girls as well as for boys; care is defined as a capacity shared by both sexes.

Again, television inherits and gives new form to the moral educational stakes of popular cinema. TV characters can be 'set loose' and opened to the imagination and usage of all, 'entrusted' to us—as if it were up to each of us to take care of them by taking care of ourselves, and, sometimes, to accept them as fundamentally unknowable, even if familiar (as with great characters like Jack Bauer). A television viewer who follows a series from the beginning might live with its characters for five or seven years or more. This is a considerable amount of time: there are few people in real life who are with us for so long. And when a new character arrives, our first reaction tends to be one of rejection, before getting to know the different facets of their personality, entering into their temporality, discovering what is important for them. It is all this work of attention and understanding that makes series into a true form of self-education, of moral learning—not in the sense of a morality lesson, but rather as a part of our progress and growth.

Thus, series must be analysed as veritable social interactions: viewers participate in them by making use of their capacities for practical reasoning, their ordinary knowledge of the world, and their moral competence. Such competence is a given (thus, it can be called ordinary), but it also needs to be constantly educated—through the efforts of a viewer well versed in various genres, through the transformations and surprises that characters hold in store for us (much more, these days, than plots do), and through the constant confrontations with the real that we find in current political series.

The concept of moral sensibility makes it possible to go beyond classical moral conceptions by approaching morality from a different angle: by focusing on people's ways of being, their natural expressions and reactions, the moving textures of personalities, the constitution of characters over the long term, the expression of a view of the world through personal discourse and style, the depiction of and appreciation for an enemy—as on *24* or *Fauda*, and the recent—and not bad—*Teheran*. Such approaches must be based on refined perception, fitting expression, and the education of sensibility. A moral attitude or competence consists in perceiving not objects or situations but rather the possibilities and meanings that emerge within things, in anticipating, improvising at each moment of perception the possibility of describing and demonstrating to the audience what is important, what matters. It is in their moral expression and way of being that a person's or character's moral vision is developed—in turn developing that of the interlocutor or viewer.

Through a 'loving and attentive' and thus caring reading, we perceive moral situations differently and actively. This changes our perception of the responsibility of the moral agent and of agency itself. The attention to others, both enjoined and creatively explored by literature and the arts, does not give us new certainties or the literary or artistic equivalent of theories. Rather, it confronts us with uncertainty and scepticism. By focusing on a narrow conception of ethics and perception, one risks missing the adventure, in Diamond's phrasing. That is, one risks missing a dimension of morality, specifically the visible aspect of moral thinking, or 'what moral life looks like'.[6] Moreover, it is owing to a lack of care that we manage to miss this all-important aspect of ethics.

Conceptual adventure is hence a component of moral perception. There is adventure in any situation that mixes uncertainty, instability, and 'the sharp sense of life'. Diamond and Nussbaum refer to a passage from James that makes beautifully explicit this adventurous form that moral life takes:

A human, personal 'adventure' is not an a priori, positive, absolute and inextinguishable thing, but just a matter of relationship and appreciation—in fact, it is a name we give, appropriately, to any passage, any situation that has added the sharp taste of uncertainty to a sharp sense of life. Hence the thing is, quite admirably, a matter of interpretation and of particular conditions; and without a perception of these, the most prodigious adventures may vulgarly count for nothing.[7]

Famous passages in James's novel *The Ambassadors* highlight this adventure of perception. The novel's hero, the sensitive, aging, sheltered Lambert Strether, comes to acquire a new moral attitude and a 'new standard of perception' in the 'great swarm' of Parisian life, which turns out to be difficult, uncertain, and dangerous. These troubling moments in the novel define caring as seeing and, conversely, attentive, and anticipatory perception as caring. Caring is activity, mobility, and improvisation as Cora Diamond notes:

> What happens to her becomes an adventure, becomes interesting, exciting, by the nature of the attention she gives it, by the intensity of her awareness, by her imaginative response. [. . .] The inattentive reader thus misses out doubly: he misses out on the adventure of the characters (for him, 'they count for nothing'), and he misses out on his own adventure as a reader.[8]

Thus, we can see moral life as an adventure that is both conceptual (one extends one's concepts) and sensory (one exposes oneself). Put another way, it is both passive (one allows oneself to be transformed, to be touched) and agentive (one seeks 'an active sense of life'). There is no need to separate conceptual life and affection, just as there is no need to separate, in moral experience, thought (spontaneity) and receptivity (vulnerability to reality and to others). James adds that it is necessary that nothing escape the attention: 'Try to be one of the people on whom nothing is lost.' With this insight, we have reached our final construal of the ethics of care and its integration into works of television.

In our times, it is arguably in film and television productions that evince the Wittgensteinian attention to detail and its proximity to care most strongly. A number of examples in recent cinema portray, through the description and fine-grained narration of caring, the agentive dimension of care within the great diversity of forms care may take. It is as if cinema, having exhausted the representations and conversations of romance (emblematized in comedies of remarriage and the melodramas of the Golden Age of Hollywood), now depicts a wider variety of forms and objects of affection. We might think of the accentuation of care in disaster or science fiction films, whose plots often centre on the preservation or survival of a family structure: *The Day After Tomorrow* (Roland Emmerich, 2004), *War of the Worlds*, *Don't Look Up* (Adam McKay, 2021). Recent TV series focus on care (*The Leftovers*, *This Is Us*), and some present the concrete work of care: *Unbelievable*, *Maid*. TV series have the capacity to highlight the necessity and importance, for all humans, of this dimension of our lives—and to shape both perception and morality together.

In TV series, care is a subject (series often portray the attitude or work of care), a means (it is something aroused, provoked), and an act (the series itself practises care). The care practised by a series is nothing spectacular; it is one of those phenomena that are seen but not noticed and which ensure the ongoing conversation and conservation of a human world. Series depict concern for others and conflicts of care. *Everwood*—whose hero, played by the excellent Treat Williams, abandons his prestigious career as a neurosurgeon after the death of his wife to practise medicine in a small town in Colorado where he has moved with his two children—depicts, in each episode, the conflicts of care that its main character must navigate (between taking care of his children, his patients, and himself) in the wake of his initial decision to choose care over career. *ER* constantly connects the demands of private life to those of work and to the conflicts internal to providing care (whether medical or moral) for patients. In a more comic style, *House*, through its highly original and forceful main character, allows for the paradoxical emergence of a form of care that is expressed in a refusal to take care of others—but which is no less effective and real. The cult series *Six Feet Under* essentially extended the domain of care to ordinary people who have died; this is also one of the meanings of the series *Cold Case*, which is entirely driven by disinterested concern for people who have disappeared. Although these series differ in style, they are all linked to care, an unavoidable subject or motif of fiction.

Care is not just a subject, because series are also means of sparking care (by awakening affectivity, representing moving characters, and creating attachments). Viewers' and fans' preoccupations with characters' fate—for example, Jon Snow's on the beloved series *Game of Thrones*—are not marginal phenomena. They reveal the true heart of TV series—the attachment to characters that we build over the years. This does not necessarily have anything to do with suspense; we may think of the example of Jack Pearson, the father on *This Is Us*, who is repeatedly shown dying, and who holds our attention although we know perfectly well that he has died and how.

The human material of TV series allows for close reading, for fully developed contextualization, for a historicity of the public and private relationship (regularity, duration), and a familiarization and education of perception (attention to the expressions and gestures of characters we come to know). Such material also makes it possible to shift the stakes of morality toward the examination of moral life, with all its difficulties and impasses, as on the famous series *Desperate Housewives*, which depicted a group of four, sometimes five, women living in a rather upscale and nondescript suburb as they grapple with extreme conflicts of care. By making characters' conflictual relationships to care (caring for children, parents, home) a central expression of their moral makeup, TV series legitimize care and give it public expression. The first episode of the first season of *ER* centres on an ordinary day in the life of Dr Greene, as previously mentioned, and shows the various demands that caring for his patients, his friends and family, and himself place on him. *Desperate Housewives* opens with a recounting of the daily household chores done by one of its heroines, whose suicide looms over the entire first season. Such scenes likely represent historical moments in the publicization of care and made possible later show openings such as that of *Better Things*, which focuses on a single mother and her three daughters, and the first episode of *This Is Us*, which succeeds in tightening our connection to its characters through its exemplary plot construction. Episodes of *The West Wing* that focused on caring for Alzheimer's patients or on the need to aid certain populations also represent high points in expressing care about care itself.

As part of reading the moral expression of series, one of the tasks of TV criticism is to demonstrate the collective and individual choices, the negotiations, conflicts, and agreements that are at the basis of moral representation: characters' choices and trajectories, plot developments, and so on. Thus, the question of morality is shifted toward interpreting public choices and developing a common sensibility, one that is both presupposed by and educated/ transformed by media forms. Of course, there can be good and bad forms of education, but an education that takes seriously a viewer's moral capacity is a good form of care. Nowadays, with political or 'security' series, this question has become even more pointed. These shows depict democracies combating terrorism and illustrate the geopolitical and political stakes of this fight and of various intelligence-gathering techniques, but they also present the point of view of the 'enemy', who is often dehumanized or caricatured (especially in film), but on these shows is depicted as doing the same job as the main characters (*24*, *Homeland*, *Fauda*, *The Bureau*, *The Looming Tower*, *Teheran*).

The characters of TV fiction are so well anchored and clear in their moral expressions that they can be made available to the imagination, affection, and usage of all. We become attached to these characters because they affect us. We are affected and concerned by what happens to them, even if it is not our own life. This affection has all the elements of an attachment, but what is truly at play in it is a moral bond, the emergence and sharing of what matters. We take care of characters and they in return take care of us by remaining a part of us after their show has ended. The final scenes of *Lost* are a reflection on how the experience of a series remains rooted in each viewer, just as the forgotten experience of the island remains buried within the characters who, within the storyline of that episode, have lived entirely different lives and never met one another.

More broadly, the great series teach us how to separate from characters to whom we have become deeply attached, sometimes by virtue of their very shortcomings (here we may think of *The Wire*, *Six Feet Under*, *Mad Men*, *Orange is The New Black*, *Better Call Saul*, and so on). Their endings, which are prepared for well in advance (and perhaps have been thought of since the beginning), testify to the true nature of our relationship to characters: it is a preparation for loss.

The ending of a series always means a painful separation, especially when we are leaving characters as strong as those on *The Americans*, one of the best series of the century. Our final, necessary separation from its main characters, Elizabeth and Philip, is expressed through one last subversion: they abandon their children and then in turn are abandoned by them. Elizabeth and Philip abandon their son to what they know will be a better life—and are abandoned by their daughter on a train platform, in one of the most wrenching scenes of the series (and, for me, of all contemporary series). It is in this moment that the series constitutes our capacity as viewers to separate from the characters and from the show itself. Stan (Elizabeth's and Philip's FBI friend) lets them go, as if to teach us too how to let them go, and how to go on without them. The characters will also go on without us, but will remain within us, taking care of us in the perverse, convoluted way that caused us to become attached to them in the first place.

This may also be to do with the uniqueness of *The Americans*; its closure is, for perhaps the only time in our 'life in series', totally open, in contrast to the highly metaphysical ending of *Six Feet Under*, which shows the inevitable death of its characters. We have absolutely no idea what will happen to Elizabeth, Philip, Paige, or Stan. This openness to the viewer's imagination and desires is one of the strengths of its ending.

It was as an experience rather than as an object that cinema interested Cavell, and this serves as the basis for an ordinary theory of cinema that can be applied to TV series, making it possible to consolidate the concrete idea of shared experience. This book and its companion, *TV-Philosophy in Action*, focus has focused on the experiential, moral, and political productivity of TV series, anchoring their content and ontology in the traditions of moral perfectionism and ordinary language philosophy. Attention to moral expression in these works is based on an articulation of cognition, perception, and expression. It is these dimensions and their interweaving that must be conceptualized, drawing on approaches (such as the philosophy of ordinary language and ethnomethodology) that have envisaged conversations and interactions as serial processes by which actions are coordinated within a given situation and meanings are made and shared. Such articulation modifies the analysis of ordinary exchanges—those centred on the expression of values—in films and television series. It finds its illustration in moral situations; that is to say, in the perception of ordinary moral situations and expressions (including the situations represented on-screen). Language is not to be considered in its descriptive function alone, nor even as agentive (performative), but as a perceptual instrument that allows for a subtlety and fine-tuning of perceptions and actions. This is ultimately what makes it possible to go beyond classical moral conceptions and to imagine different moral approaches: focusing on people's ways of being, their natural expressions and reactions, the moving texture of personalities, the constitution of characters over time, the expression of a vision of the world through speech and personal style. It is in public moral expression (choice of words, style of conversation) that a person's or character's moral vision and form of life is developed, in turn modifying the viewer's or interlocuter's. In the end this radically transforms the meaning of 'reception': to be transformed and affected by these interactions, one must also be active. TV series and their morality are thus new sites of viewers' agency.

For Cavell, as for Dewey, the value of culture lies in its capacity to transform us: 'In this light, philosophy becomes the education of grownups . . . The anxiety in teaching, in serious communication, is that I myself require education. And for grownups this is not natural growth, but *change*.'[9] Cavell calls this philosophical undertaking 'moral education', or 'pedagogy', as in the subtitle to *Cities of Words: Pedagogical Letters on a Register of the Moral Life*. This pedagogical claim regarding the task of philosophy recalls Dewey's involvement in the science of education. For both authors, the educational value of popular culture is more than anecdotal; it defines how both 'popular' and 'culture' (in the sense of *Bildung*) ought to be understood in the expression 'popular culture'. Popular culture does not refer to a primitive or inferior version of culture, but rather to a shared democratic form of life that creates common values and serves as a resource for a form of self-education. More specifically, it is a form of culture of the self, a subjective perfecting or subjectivation that occurs through sharing and commenting on ordinary and public material that is integrated into ordinary life.

My claim is that what Cavell claimed for Hollywood popular movies—their capacity to create a culture shared by millions, beyond the USA—has been transferred onto TV series, which have taken up, if not taken over, the task of educating us. Cavell's argument in *Cities of Words* was perfectionist, redefining morality in new terms—no longer in terms of 'the good' or rational judgement, but rather the exploration of forms of life where humans are searching for better selves. For Cavell, there is an affinity between cinema—good movies—and a particular understanding of the good, an understanding that is foreign to so-called dominant moral theories. The importance and benefit of extending this perfectionism to include TV series is equally ethical, for these works are as shared and public as movies were, in Cavell's eye, in the twentieth century; they reach a significant audience and play an educational role, and they make it possible at last to anchor the value of a work in the experience one has of it.

Cavell's ordinary aesthetics deliberately goes against the traditional critical approach, where there is an obsession with art as a separate domain—a view admirably criticized by Dewey—and with the mystique of the individual creator, as well as with representation and image, to the detriment of the ordinary experience of seeing a movie, which is the subjective—but always shared—experience of public material.

The forms of popular culture that interest me here are those that are capable of transforming our existence by educating and cultivating our ordinary experience, not only in the classical sense of training our aesthetic taste, but also in the sense of a moral training that is constitutive of our singularity. Cavell, combining Emerson's analyses (in his essay 'Experience') and Dewey's (in his chapter 'Having an Experience' in *Art as Experience*),[10] emphasizes that it is important to be able to educate one's experience in such a way that one can have confidence in it, and in this way to live it. Cinephilia is a form of education of the self, and seriphilia is even more so. This education does not occur through exposure to a set of universal masterpieces (even if such TV classics do now exist), but through the constitution of one's personal list of favourite movies or series and of scenes that are appropriate to various circumstances or occasions of one's life, when they are remobilized.

The question, again, is what the ordinary does to philosophy. The total cinematographic art, whether in the form of movies or TV series or other new genres, is 'popular' art because experiencing it underlies ordinary experience, just as Dewey maintained that aesthetic experience is emblematic of experience in general. This experience is *moral*—both mysterious and ordinary, personal and public. It is ordinary because nothing is more shareable and self-evident than going to see movies or watching shows and talking about them, with these often being the moments when we re-enact our agreement in language. This coming to know what counts for oneself is a mysterious form of knowledge, and there is nothing easy or immediate about it. The only source for verifying one's understanding of what counts is *oneself*—whence the role of confidence, of trust in one's own experience,[11] which is the source of moral perfectionism and the only basis for public education.

We may remember that Martin Sheen, who played the mythical President Bartlet on the beloved *The West Wing*, was so popular in 2000 that an NBC poll placed him ahead of George W. Bush and Al Gore in the presidential election. *he Handmaid's Tale*, too, anticipated today's fearsome attacks on women's rights. *La Casa de Papel* offered words and sounds for the mobilizations of the last years. Series sometimes even anticipate threats, as *Homeland* did, when, in its fifth season, written in 2014, it portrayed European jihadist terrorist cells. When the show was broadcast, the day after the November 2015 attacks in Paris, the creators changed the dialogue to include the attacks that had just struck the French capital. *Chernobyl* should be revisited today as nuclear power plants are being bombed and nuclear energy is less and less a topic of public discussion.

Israeli series have been trailblazers in representing a state of insecurity in which one must lead an ordinary life. Series and mainstream movies have acknowledged this state of affairs by representing and expressing the threats and risks that make up the current security context. Series' influence is not limited to only one country or area: current revolutions in the modes of production, distribution, and consumption of these fictions encourage circulation between cultural zones. The porousness of the boundaries between the factual and the fictional facilitates the integration of these fictions into understandings of the world, systems of knowledge, and ways of envisioning a shared future. TV series shape common understandings of the controversial topic of security . . . and they travel, as Israeli series do in the most outstanding way.

The importance that intangible components of power—so-called soft power—have taken on over the past thirty years constitutes an obvious transformation in forms of war. Information warfare, influence, manipulation, and counter-propaganda are at the heart of strategies to counter, for example, propaganda from the Islamic State. Though forms of soft power may seek to use fictional representations of terrorism to attempt to influence the enemy's decision-making processes or as forms of internal propaganda, movies and TV series can play a subtler, significant, and so far under-studied role in shaping scholarly analysis, education, and collective understandings of terrorist violence.

Thus far, these cultural objects have been ignored as negligible and as mere entertainment, or analysed through the lens of propaganda, influence, and manipulation. What has been missing until now is a more nuanced and exhaustive account of their impact on both the public and on defence actors, and of the consequences and risks of this impact. Filling in this gap means taking into account and demonstrating their degree of reflexivity, and their integration of the audience's moral capabilities.

Popular fiction is taken seriously by national security institutions: a few days after the 9/11 attacks, the CIA initiated a series of meetings with film and TV creators (directors, screenwriters, producers) to help the agency imagine future attack scenarios and anticipate threats. Security institutions (defence, intelligence) are opening up to the entertainment industry in Europe. In 2016, the French minister of defence Jean-Yves Le Drian announced the launch of a 'Mission Cinéma' to encourage fiction creators to focus on subjects connected to the defence world. In 1948, the Pentagon created a liaison office with Hollywood—a move the CIA imitated in 1996, not without controversy, in order to increase the realism of film and TV productions as well as to improve the agency's public image and attract new recruits (a good example of the results of this liaison is the character Sydney Bristow, played by Jennifer Garner). Security series open viewers to sympathy/empathy with characters at first seen as 'enemies', and to difficult, no-win moral choices and situations. In representing terrorism and counter-terrorism in action, these fictions give audiences a specific experience of the contemporary security world. They can be seen as attempts at collective reflection, as a democratic inquiry into an increasingly complex reality. They give unprecedented visibility to a dimension of democratic life usually hidden from the public: secrecy, espionage, the 'reason of state' in action. The images of reality and fiction produced since the beginning of the century and 9/11 have together constructed representations, affects, and politics, creating a new realism. The 'security' films and series that followed that event—and sometimes preceded and heralded it—are not effects or by-products of it: they constituted it and continue to do so. For 9/11 is not an archived, patrimonialized image of the past.

If the 2001 attacks are often left out of serial fiction, with the exception of *Homeland*, the effects (real or supposed) of 9/11 on democracies continue to saturate the fictional space. Terrorism, intelligence, and espionage continue to fascinate, as does the risk of deterioration of democratic regimes under the effects of counter-terrorism and a drift towards prioritizing security over all else. The 2001 attacks are conceived primarily as an emergence of the unexpected—despite the previous attack on the World Trade Center in 1993, as well as the rise of the jihadist threat embodied by Al-Qaeda that might have made these attacks conceivable, if not foreseeable. Can TV shows help us prevent attacks? This is the meaning of the notion of a 'failure of imagination' put forth in the report by the bipartisan 9/11 Commission: the inability to anticipate the event, not only because of the technical and political ingenuity of the terrorists, but also because of the sin of pride (which is inherent in the question 'Why do 'they' hate 'us'?' with which the post-attack debate was occupied). The thesis of a lack of imagination, which is theoretically attractive, is nonetheless limited: it avoids the numerous problems of inter-service cooperation, the question of responsibilities, and the strategic errors at the origin of the attacks—in this case an inability to understand the enemy and to take the threat seriously. The series *The Looming Tower* gives a clear idea of the unpreparedness of the American security forces: the impressive character of Ali Soufan, a real-life agent played by the wonderful actor Tahar Rahim, is presented as one of only eight Arabic speakers in the FBI before the attacks. You don't need imagination—just knowledge, realism, and thought.

Well, Sheen has never been president of the United States, nor has the excellent Dennis Haysbert, who premonitorily incarnated David Palmer in *24*. President Zelensky, on the other hand, has become the showrunner of the fate of Ukraine, starting with his show *Servant of the People*—a series that offered him the role of his life and allowed him to move from 'soft power' to hard power. Actually, Yuri Kostyuk, the main screenwriter of the *Servant of the People* series, has been for the past four years the president's speechwriter. He has described his job in baffling terms:

> We are given the theme one or two weeks in advance. we meet in the president's office. The president himself makes a small pitch, we think together, and then we get to work. . . . We have kept our habits as screenwriters: you target, you build your text to reach the audience.[12]

This is a new species of realism; not only reality impacted by fiction, and conversely, but reality built with the tools of fiction.

The look and feel of *Servant of the People* owe a great deal to *The West Wing*, and the show is soaked in American democratic culture; Goloborodko, Zelensky's character, reminds us of Capra's John Doe or Longfellow Deeds. TV series create a new public space and a form of democratic life, collectively elaborated. They are not only a resource for reflection on the stakes of the present moment, but also a tool for moral, social, and political transformation. Education through series represents new hope in a world where fake anti-democratic values are implemented or promoted by many regimes and political actors, and where political discourses and commitments are sometimes emptied of their meaning. TV series now have such a place in the lives of viewers that they cannot be reduced to merely, as some used to say, 'a mirror of society'. They also have a specific agency in and on the world—for a start, through the transformations they produce in us.

TV series, even when they claim realism, discuss and illustrate moral perfectionism. They claim their capacity to analyse and criticize reality, while giving voice and space to new categories of humans. Attention to ordinary expression within these corpora leads to reconsidering the question of suffocated or neglected female expression, which found a voice first in popular cinema and then in TV series: see *Desperate Housewives, Buffy, Dollhouse, Top of the Lake, The Handmaid's Tale, Big Little Lies, Unbelievable, Maid*. The series *For All Mankind* introduces fictitious female characters who are involved in the early conquest of space, as well as black characters, thus deploying and opening up the casting of *Mankind*, but also the concept of mankind. Series also often do the work of reparation (*When They See Us*, *Unbelievable*, *Lupin*, *Maid*, etc.) that popular cinema has sometimes failed to do but that the hybrid format of single-season series seems to explore. To achieve these goals, series create their own mythologies on the model of the contemporary myths, of which *Star Wars* is a great model (although the quality of the franchise declined somewhat in series, it also allowed for its own inventions, in particular through a significant cast of actors). Exploiting the privilege of the serial timeframe and the diachronic complexity of their characters, TV series enter the fields of metaphysics and scepticism, posing questions about mortality, sexuality, and human/non-human and living/non-living differences. Finally, during the pandemic, a prelude to other crises to come, series took care of their audiences, reciprocating the relationship of care that the viewers have had for years with their characters. In the midst of the COVID-19 crisis, they invented and elicited forms of resilience, via the renewed visibility and significance of the ongoing risk of terrorism, seen as the paradigm for other crises and threats. By showing vulnerable and fallible humans that we come to care about, series emerge as an art for a vulnerable world.

A theoretical discussion of TV series is pointless if it is not engaged in an analysis of what series do to us, as well as in the study of particular series. Although I have emphasized how classic series constitute our personal and collective history, our corpus, and our culture, I am also interested in tracing the singular experience and the political and moral, sometimes metaphysical, impact of the series that have formed and shaped us in recent years, while also (in)forming new meanings of 'us' (hence the strong presence of the series *This Is Us* in my corpus).[13]

The format of series we are dealing with here has revealed itself as an aesthetic form of the democratic ideal. Meanwhile, moral exploration is at the heart of most TV shows rooted in everyday life. By allowing each viewer to increase the intensity of their lives and understanding of their own potential, series present us with a form of democratic life that is no longer based on pre-existing and consensual values, but is rooted in inventing shareable values through the possibilities of the medium.

Notes

1   Glévarec, *La sériephilie*, p. 99.
2   Ibid., p. 103.
3   Cavell, *The World Viewed*, p. 154.
4   Sabine Chalvon-Demersay, "Des personnages de si près tenus", TV Fiction and Moral Consensus', *Qualitative Sociology Review* 3, no. 3 (2007): 6–21.
5   Chalvon-Demersay, 'Enquête sur l'étrange nature du héros de série télévisée', p. 212.
6   Diamond, *The Realistic Spirit*, p. 36.

7   Henry James, 'The Art of Fiction', in *Theory of Fiction*, edited by E. James and M. Lincoln, Jr (Lincoln: University of Nebraska Press, 1972), p. 307.

8   Cora Diamond, *The Realistic Spirit*, pp. 314–315.

9   Cavell, *The Claim of Reason*, p. 125.

10   Dewey, *Art as Experience*, 10.

11   Cavell, *Pursuits of Happiness*, p. 12; Dewey, *Art as Experience*, ch. 3.

12   *Le Monde*, interview by Ariane Chemin, February 2023.

13   See the companion volume, *TV-Philosophy in Action* (University of Exeter Press, 2023).

Conclusion: Hope against Hope

Twin Peaks will not have a fourth season. *The Americans*, perhaps the most poignant series of the twenty-first century so far, ended by affirming its status as a classic through the pain it caused in separating us from its heroes—but also by leaving the destiny of all its characters, Elizabeth, Philip, as well as Paige, Henry, and Stan, open to our imagination and attention. *The Leftovers*, arguably the most original and disturbing work to appear this century, also ended in 2017 by, rather curiously, becoming the paradigm for apocalyptic series well beyond its fanatical audience—we witness a reprise of this, for example, in the aesthetics of the final minutes of the blockbuster *Avengers: Infinity War* (Anthony Russo and Joe Russo, 2018), in which a notable portion of the superheroes (even the young Spiderman) fade away without explanation.

Homeland, the iconic security series that revolutionized the genre, is also over, as is *The Walking Dead*, which has gone a long way in its education of adults (another name for philosophy) and in bringing us face to face with the transformations we have undergone by frequenting this universe where values are gradually erased in a conversational mode.

Game of Thrones has completed its final season and, while it has already sparked a feeling of exhaustion in anticipation of its coming spin-offs, it remains the series that has given rhythm to our lives over the course of the past decade and proved our capacity to integrate unlikeable characters into our lives. In any case, it is the end of an era: *This Is Us* and *Ozark*, which continued over the past few years to magnificently illustrate the classic narrative form of the ensemble family series, both came to an end in 2022, and *For All Mankind* and *The Crown*, for historical/ontological reasons, will soon reach the present moment and conclude.

Fortunately, we can count on non-American series, whether French (*Baron Noir, Hippocrate, En Thérapie*), English, German, Israeli (*Fauda, False Flag, Teheran*), or Korean (*Squid Game*), whose good health seems to indicate where the dynamism of seriphilia lies today. American productions, while they still offer excitement, have become less universal—they are increasingly disseminated as niche products or miniseries (six to ten episodes).

In any case, it seems reasonable to think that there are no successors to the model of the 'waves' of great series of the 1990s, 2000s (*The Sopranos, The Wire, The Shield, Lost, Six Feet Under, Mad Men, Breaking Bad* etc.), or 2010s (*The Americans, House of Cards, Homeland, Game of Thrones, The Walking Dead,*

Vikings, Breaking Bad, The Leftovers, Narcos, Better Call Saul, This is Us, etc.) that I sought to retrace at the opening of this book. And this is despite the depressing proliferation of Netflix products that use targeted writing to try to combine the most 'successful' models, parasitically feeding off the great heritage of TV series.

Will the popular television series suffer the same fate as cinema, which has not had any great global successes in the twenty-first century apart from franchises, sequels, sagas—in short, 'series' of movies? Will television series, born in the second half of the twentieth century and revolutionized at the beginning of the next with works of considerable importance, be only a short-lived moment lasting a few decades in the history of Western cultures? Indeed, am I just reprising Cavell's gesture and mood in *The World Viewed*, when he expresses the view that cinema as he had loved it for decades is over, and tries to capture how it has mattered to him?

This heritage, and all these great works that make TV shows deserving of the title of art (I have named a good number of them, and it is up to each of you to complete your own lists according to your own ideas—the one and only lesson of this book being that each of us is the authority on our own personal culture) are, in terms of their cultural significance, similar to the great novels of the nineteenth and twentieth centuries, which perhaps serve as a more appropriate model than the cinema.

As I have argued, the democratic power of series—both in their reach and the transformative potential of their content, is formidable despite the considerable number of undemocratic governments in the world today. Series continue to signal and support democratic aspiration through their capacity to educate audiences and to disseminate distant, obscure and even bizarre ideas, life forms and cultures, which make them potent tools in future struggles for the creation of alternative systems of widely shared values. This is the 'democratization of perfectionism' that is characteristic of other forms of popular culture: it is culture that continues to be the site of conversations about the society in which we live. As Cavell said of cinema, 'If there are people who continue to make such works for an audience of friends and strangers, works that help us to imagine the possibility of exchange between human beings, who knows what else we can hope for?'[1]

We might also look at the list of new series being talked about around the world. As I have just mentioned, North America no longer has a monopoly on creativity in the field of television series—with the latest ones to make their mark including French, Spanish, Korean, Israeli, Senegalese, Indian, Polish, Turkish, and German productions. Netflix's dominance has not changed this, and in fact represents another aspect of the democratization of series in light of the way it has nurtured local creations. While this is counterbalanced to some extent by the drive towards a level of conformity to suit global audiences, with the consequent enlargement of the potential target audience, a 'local' series can reach provides hitherto unimagined opportunities for such products to circulate internationally. Television series have played a large part in subverting the domination of Hollywood and the English-speaking norm.

Another interesting phenomenon is that TV series, despite their diversity, tend to be ideologically more or less of a piece in this century, similar to the way Hollywood movies of all genres were during the New Deal years, when Emersonian perfectionism was ascendant in Hollywood, as it was across the United States. In this way, TV series have inherited the moral agenda of film. Today, you would have a hard time finding a show that isn't progressivist, feminist, and offering moral hope of some kind to the next generations.

The invention of cinema constituted a radical transformation of people's lives, the end of what Dewey called the 'chasm between ordinary and aesthetic experience'.[2] Following in its wake, TV series have made possible a new form of revolution in our lives: the redistribution of public and private space that occurs when that which is public becomes intimate, and that which is private is exposed; a revolution brought about by the mutations of life in which film and TV are inextricably embedded.

Television series have accompanied our ordinary lives over the years, and they have proven to be a resource or refuge, especially in extraordinary situations, offering universes of comfort. They have offered a semblance of continuity amidst the upheaval of the pandemic, with its prohibition on public space. Their increased prominence in our lives at this time empowered them to take care of us during lockdown. This serial care can be seen as an essential part of our collective moral survival.

As a result of the history of their inception, series have almost never been accessible in public cinemas, and this has played an important part in how they have been valued. They were long underestimated as a format connected to private life—a sphere associated with the feminine—and thus devalued by cinephiles. Their reception took place not in cinemas, open to the public, but in the domestic universe, where a television set was a piece of furniture and the audience was typically female. Series were historically constructed as a minor medium, whose preferred subject matter was the private sphere, and close relationships. Their revalorization epitomizes shifts in the boundaries between private and public life. It was in shifting to the depiction of professional universes (medical, legal, police) that televised series acquired first social, then political relevance. They have become more and more wide-ranging, thus metaphorically entering the public space. Now they are a public space in their own right. In this way, television series have a power of their own, a thought of their own: they provoke and shape thought about the world in which we live.

Notes

1   Cavell, Preface to the French volume *Le cinéma nous rend-il meilleurs?* (Paris: Bayard, 2003; Vrin, 2023.

2   *Art as Experience*, 10.

Bibliography

Austin, J. L., *Philosophical Papers*, second edition (Oxford: Clarendon Press, 1970).

Boggs, Carl, and Tom Pollard, *The Hollywood War Machine: U.S. Militarism and Popular Culture* (New York: Routledge, 2017).

Bourdieu, Emmanuel, 'Stanley Cavell—Pour Une Esthétique d'un Art Impur', in *Stanley Cavell: Cinema et Philosophie*, edited by Marc Cerisuelo and Sandra Laugier (Paris: Presses de la Sorbonne Nouvelle, 2000), 43-60.

Boutet, Marjolaine, *Cold Case (Meredith Stiehm, CBS, 2003–2010): La mélodie du passé* (Paris: Presses Universitaires de France, 2013).

Brunsdon, Charlotte, 'Bingeing on Box-Sets: The National and the Digital in Television Crime Drama', in *Relocating Television. Television in the Digital Context*, edited by Jostein Gripsrud, first edition, pp. 63–75 (London and New York: Routledge, 2010).

Cavell, Stanley, *A Pitch of Philosophy: Autobiographical Exercises* (Cambridge, MA: Harvard University Press, 1994).

———, *Cavell on Film*, edited by William Rothman (New York: SUNY Press, 2005).

———, *Cities of Words: Pedagogical Letters on a Register of the Moral Life* (Cambridge, MA: Belknap Press of Harvard University Press, 2004).

———, *Contesting Tears: The Hollywood Melodrama of the Unknown Woman* (Chicago: University of Chicago Press, 1996).

———, *In Quest of the Ordinary: Lines of Skepticism and Romanticism* (Chicago: University of Chicago Press, 1988).

———, *Little Did I Know: Excerpts from Memory* (Stanford, CA: Stanford University Press, 2010).

———, *Must We Mean What We Say?: A Book of Essays* (Cambridge: Cambridge University Press, 1969).

———, *Pursuits of Happiness: The Hollywood Comedy of Remarriage* (Cambridge, MA: Harvard University Press, 1981).

———, 'Something out of the Ordinary', *Proceedings and Addresses of the American Philosophical Association* 71, no. 2 (1997): 23–37, https://doi.org/10.2307/3130939.

———, *The Claim of Reason: Wittgenstein, Skepticism, Morality, and Tragedy* (Oxford: Oxford University Press, 1979).

———, 'The Fact of Television', *Daedalus* 111, no. 4 (1982): 75–96.

————, *The Senses of Walden*, expanded edition (Chicago: University of Chicago Press, 1992).

————, 'The Thought of Movies', in *Themes out of School: Effects and Causes*, 3–26 (Chicago: University of Chicago Press, 1988).

————, *The World Viewed: Reflections on the Ontology of Film*, enlarged edition (Cambridge, MA, and London: Viking Press, 1971).

————, 'What Becomes of Things on Film?', *Philosophy and Literature* 2, no. 2 (1978): 249–57, https://doi.org/10.1353/phl.1978.0027.

Chalvon-Demersay, Sabine, '"Des personnages de si près tenus", TV Fiction and Moral Consensus', *Qualitative Sociology Review* 3, no. 3 (2007): 6–21.

————, 'Enquête sur l'étrange nature du héros de série télévisée', *Réseaux* 165, no. 1 (2011): 181–214.

————, 'La confusion des conditions. Une enquête sur la série télévisée Urgences', *Réseaux. Communication – Technologie – Société* 17, no. 95 (1999): 235–83, https://doi.org/10.3406/reso.1999.2160.

Clémot, Hugo, *Cinéthique* (Paris: Vrin, 2018).

Corner, John, *Critical Ideas in Television Studies* (Oxford: Clarendon Press, 1999).

Dewey, John, *Art as Experience* (New York: Perigee, 1980).

————, *The Public and Its Problems* (New York: Henry Holt and Company, 1927).

Diamond, Cora, *The Realistic Spirit: Wittgenstein, Philosophy, and the Mind*, reprint (Cambridge, MA: MIT Press, 1995 [1991]).

Emerson, Ralph Waldo, *The Essential Writings of Ralph Waldo Emerson*, edited by Brooks Atkinson (New York: Modern Library, 2000).

Engell, Lorenz, *Thinking Through Television* (Amsterdam: Amsterdam University Press, 2019).

————, *The Switch Image: Television Philosophy*, Thinking Media, book 9 (New York: Bloomsbury Academic, 2021).

Ferrarese, Estelle, and Sandra Laugier (eds), *Formes de vie* (Paris: CNRS, 2018).

Fiske, John, *Television Culture* (London and New York: Routledge, 1989).

Flitterman-Lewis, Sandy, 'All's Well That Doesn't End—Soap Opera and the Marriage Motif', *Camera Obscura* (1988): 118–27.

Frye, Northrop, *Anatomy of Criticism* (Princeton, NJ: Princeton University Press, 2020).

Gefen, A. and S. Laugier (eds), *Le pouvoir des liens faibles* (Paris: CNRS editions, 2020).

Glévarec, Hervé, *La sériephilie: sociologie d'un attachement culturel et place de la fiction dans la vie des jeunes adultes* (Paris: Ellipses, 2012).

Jenkins, Tricia, *The CIA in Hollywood: How the Agency Shapes Film and Television* (Austin: University of Texas Press, 2016).

Kavka, Misha, *Reality Television, Affect and Intimacy. Reality Matters* (Houndmills: Palgrave, 2008).

Krauss, Rosalind E., 'Rosalind Krauss on Dark Glasses and Bifocals'. *Artforum* 12, no. 9 (May 1974): 59–62.

LaRocca, David and Sandra Laugier (eds) *Television with Stanley Cavell in Mind*, Exeter: University of Exeter Press, 2023.

Laugier, Sandra (ed.), *Ethique, littérature, vie humaine* (Paris: Presses universitaires de France, 2006).

—— (ed.), *La voix et la vertu. Variétés du perfectionnisme moral* (Paris: PUF, 2010).

——, *Why We Need Ordinary Language Philosophy*, translated by Daniela Ginsburg (Chicago: University of Chicago Press, 2013).

——, 'Popular Cultures, Ordinary Criticism: A Philosophy of Minor Genres', *MLN* 127, no. 5 (2012): 997–1012.

——, 'Spoilers, Twists, and Dragons: Popular Narrative after Game of Thrones', in *Stories: Screen Narrative in the Digital Era*, edited by Ian Christie and Annie van den Oever, pp. 143–52 (Amsterdam: Amsterdam University Press, 2018).

——, 'The Conception of Film for the Subject of Television: Moral Education of the Public and a Return to an Aesthetics of the Ordinary', in *The Thought of Stanley Cavell and Cinema: Turning Anew to the Ontology of Film a Half-Century after The World Viewed*, edited by David LaRocca (London: Bloomsbury, 2020).

——, *Nos Vies en Séries: Philosophie et Morale D'une Culture Populaire*. Paris: Climats Flammarion, 2019.

Laugier, Sandra, and Marc Cerisuelo (eds), *Stanley Cavell, cinéma et philosophie* (Paris: Presses de la Sorbonne Nouvelle, 2001).

Mittell, Jason, 'The Qualities of Complexity: Vast versus Dense Seriality in Contemporary Television', in *Television Aesthetics and Style*, edited by Jason Jacobs and Steven Peacock, pp. 45–56 (New York: Bloomsbury Academic, 2013).

Modleski, Tania, 'The Rhythms of Reception: Daytime Television and Women's Work', in *Regarding Television: Critical Approaches - An Anthology*, edited by E. Ann Kaplan, pp. 67–75 (Los Angeles: American Film Institute, 1983).

Morley, David, *Television, Audiences & Cultural Studies* (London and New York: Routledge, 1992).

Mulhall, Stephen, *On Film* (London: Routledge, 2001).

Mumford, Laura Stempel, 'How Things End: The Problem of Closure on Daytime Soap Opera', *Quarterly Review of Film and Video* 15 (1994): 57–74.

Murdoch, Iris, 'On "God" and "Good"', in *Existentialists and Mystics: Writings on Philosophy and Literature*, edited by Iris Murdoch and Peter J. Conradi, pp. 76–98 (London: Chatto & Windus, 1997).

——, 'Vision and Choice in Morality', in *Existentialists and Mystics: Writings on Philosophy and Literature*, edited by Iris Murdoch and Peter J. Conradi, pp. 76–98 (London: Chatto & Windus, 1997).

Nannicelli, Ted, *Appreciating the Art of Television: A Philosophical Perspective* (London: Routledge, 2017).

Newcomb, Horace, and Paul M. Hirsch, 'Television as a Cultural Forum', in *Television. A Critical View (6th Edition)*, edited by Horace Newcomb, pp. 561–73 (New York and Oxford: Oxford University Press, 2000.

Newcomb, Horace M., 'Post-Network Television—From Flow to Publishing, from Forum to Library', in *Bildschirm-Medien-Theorien*, edited by Peter Gendolla, Peter Ludes, and Volker Roloff, pp. 33–44 (Munich: Fink, 2001).

Nussbaum, Martha, '"Finely Aware and Richly Responsible": Moral Attention and the Moral Task of Literature', *The Journal of Philosophy* 82, no. 10 (1985): 516–29, https://doi.org/10.2307/2026358.

———, *Love's Knowledge: Essays on Philosophy and Literature* (New York: Oxford University Press, 1990).

Ogien, Albert, and Sandra Laugier, *Le principe démocratie: enquête sur les nouvelles formes du politique* (Paris: Découverte, 2014).

———, *Pourquoi désobéir en démocratie?* (Paris: Éditions de la Découverte, 2010).

Paperman, Patricia, and Sandra Laugier (eds), *Le Souci des autres: éthique et politique du care* (Paris: Éditions de l'Écoles des hautes études en sciences sociales, 2005).

Pasquier, Dominique, 'La 'culture populaire' à l'épreuve des débats sociologiques', *Hermès, La Revue* 42, no. 2 (2005): 60–69, https://doi.org/10.4267/2042/8983.

———, 'Performances collectives: la réception des séries sentimentales par les jeunes téléspectateurs', *Protée* 30, no. 1 (2002): 67–78.

Robb, David L., *Operation Hollywood: How the Pentagon Shapes and Censors the Movies* (Amherst, NY: Prometheus Books, 2004).

Rodowick, D.N., *Philosophy's Artful Conversation* (Cambridge, MA: Harvard University Press, 2015).

Rothman, William, 'Cavell on Film, Television, and Opera', in *Stanley Cavell*, edited by Richard Eldridge, pp. 206–38 (Cambridge: Cambridge University Press, 2003).

Rothman, William, *The 'I' of the camera, Essays in Film Criticism, History, and Aesthetics*, second edition (Cambridge: Cambridge University Press, 2004 [1988]).

———, *Must We Kill the Thing We Love?—Emersonian Perfectionism and the Films of Alfred Hitchcock* (New York: Columbia University Press, 2014).

Saint Maurice, Thibaut de, *Philosophie en séries* (Paris: Ellipses, 2015).

———, 'Portrait du sériephile en philosophe', in *Le pouvoir des liens faibles*, edited by Alexandre Gefen and Sandra Laugier (Paris: CNRS, 2020).

Shuster, Martin, *New Television: The Aesthetics and Politics of a Genre*, illustrated edition (Chicago: University of Chicago Press, 2017).

Silverstone, Roger, *Television and Everyday Life* (London and New York: Routledge, 1994).

Sinnerbrink, Robert, *Cinematic Ethics: Exploring Ethical Experience through Film* (London and New York: Routledge, 2016).

Warshow, Robert, *The Immediate Experience: Movies, Comics, Theatre & Other Aspects of Popular Culture*, enlarged edition (Cambridge, MA: Harvard University Press, 2001).

Wittgenstein, Ludwig, *Philosophical Investigations*, translated by G.E.M. Anscombe (Englewood Cliffs, NJ: Prentice Hall, 1958).

Serigraphy and Filmography

24 (Joel Surnow & Robert Cochran, Fox, 2001–2014)
The Affair (Sarah Treem & Hagai Levi, Showtime, 2014–2019)
Alias (J.J. Abrams, ABC, 2001–2006)
The Americans (Joe Weisberg, FX, 2013–2018)
American Crime (John Ridley, ABC, 2015–2017)
Angel (Joss Whedon, WB, 1999–2004)
Annette (Leos Carax, 2021)
Baron Noir (Ziad Doueiri, Canal+, 2016–)
Barry (Alec Berg & Bill Hader, HBO, 2018–)
Better Things (Pamela Adlon, Louis C.K, FX, 2015–2022)
Big Little Lies (David E. Kelley, HBO, 2017–2019)
Borgen (Adam Price, DR1, 2010–2013)
Breaking Bad (Vince Gilligan, AMC, 2008–2013)
Buffy the Vampire Slayer (Joss Whedon, UPN, 1997–2003)
The Bureau/Le Bureau des légendes (Eric Rochant, Canal+, 2015–2021)
Chernobyl (Craig Mazin, HBO, 2019)
Cold Case (Meredith Stiehm, CBS, 2003–2010)
Columbo (Levinson & Link, NBC, 1968–2003)
The Crown (Peter Morgan, Netflix, 2016–)
Dallas (David Jacobs, CBS, 1978–1991)
Deadwood (David Milch, HBO, 2004–2006)
Designated Survivor (David Guggenheim, ABC/Netflix, 2016–2019)
Desperate Housewives (Marc Cherry, ABC, 2004–2012)
The Deuce (George Pelecanos and David Simon, HBO, 2017–2019)
Deutschland 83, 86, 89 (Anna Winger & Joerg Winger, AMC, 2015–2020)
Dexter (James Manos, Showtime, 2006–2013)
Dollhouse (Joss Whedon, Fox, 2009–2010)
Dragnet (Jack Webb, TV14, 1951–1959)
Dream On (Martha Kauffman and David Crane, HBO, 1990–1996)
Dynasty (Richard and Esther Shapiro, ABC, 1981–1989)
En Thérapie (Toledano & Nakache, Arte, 2021–). See *BeTipul*
Engrenages / Spiral (Anne Landois et al., Canal+, 2005–2020)
ER (Michael Crichton, NBC, 1994–2009)
Everwood (Greg Berlanti, The WB, 2002–2006)
False Flag (Maria Feldman and Amit Cohen, Channel 2, 2015–)

Fauda (Lior Raz and Ravi Issacharoff, Yes Oh/ Netflix, 2015–2020)

For All Mankind (Moore, Wolpert, Nedivi, Apple TV, 2019–)

Friends (Martha Kauffman and David Crane, NBC, 1994–2004)

Game of Thrones (David Benioff and D.B. Weiss, HBO, 2011–2019)

Girls (Lena Dunham, HBO, 2011–2017)

The Handmaid's Tale (Bruce Miller, Hulu, 2017–)

Hannibal (Bryan Fuller, NBC, 2013–2015)

Hatufim (Gideon Raff, Aroutz 2, 2010–2012)

High Fidelity (Nick Hornby, Hulu, 2020)

Hill Street Blues (Stephen Bochco and Mark Frost, NBC, 1981–1987)

Hippocrate (Thomas Lilti, Canal+, 2018–)

Homeland (Howard Gordon & Alex Gansa, Showtime, 2011–2020)

House (David Shore, Fox, 2004–2012)

House of Cards (Beau Willimon, Netflix, 2013–2018)

How I Met Your Mother (Bays & Thomas, CBS, 2005–2014)

I Love Lucy (Asher, Kern, Daniels, Levy, CBS, 1951–1957)

I May Destroy You (Michaela Coel, BBC One, HBO 2020)

Je te promets (TF1, 2021–)

Justified (Graham Yost, FX, 2010–2015)

Kalifat (Netflix, 2020)

Killing Eve (Phoebe Waller-Bridge and alii, BBC, 2018–2022)

The L Word (Chaiken, Abbot, & Greenberg, Showtime, 2004–2009)

La Casa de Papel (Alex Pina, Netflix, 2017–2021)

LA Law (Steven Bochco, NBC, 1986–1994)

The Leftovers (Lindelof & Perrotta, HBO, 2014–2017)

The Looming Tower (Futterman, Gibney, & Wright, Hulu, 2018)

Lost (Lieber, Abrams & Lindelof, ABC, 2004–2010)

Lupin (George Kay & François Uzan, Netflix, 2021–)

MacGuyver (Lee David Zlotoff, ABC, 1985–1992)

Mad Men (Matthew Weiner, AMC, 2007–2015)

Magnum P.I. (Bellisario & Larson, CBS, 1980–1988)

Maid (Land, Molly Smith Metzler, Netflix, 2021)

Miami Vice (Anthony Yerkoich, NBC, 1984–1989)

Modern Family (Christopher Lloyd, ABC, 2009–2020)

Moneyball (Bennett Miller, 2011)

Moonlighting (Glenn Gordon Caron, NBC, 1985–1989)

Murder One (Steven Bochco, ABC, 1995–1997)

Narcos (Brancaro, Miaro & Bernard, Netflix, 2015–2018)

Nurse Jackie (Linda Wallem, Evan Dunsky and Liz Brixius, Showtime, 2009–2015)

NYPD Blue (Steven Bochco and David Milch, ABC, 1993–2005)

Occupied (Jo Nesbo, Eric Skojoldbjaerg and Karianne Lund, TV2, 2015–2019)

Orange Is the New Black (Jenji Kohan, Netflix, 2013–2019)

Oz (Tom Fontana, HBO, 1997–2003)

Ozark (Chris Mundy, Netflix, 2017–2022)
The Persuaders (Robert S. Baker, ITV/ABC, 1971–1972)
Peyton Place (Paul Monash, NBC)
Quantum Leap (Donald P. Bellisario, NBC, 1989–1993)
Seinfeld (Larry David and Jerry Seinfeld, NBC, 1989–1998)
Servant of the People (Volodymyr Zelensky, Kvartal 95 Studio, 2015–2019)
Sex and the City (Darren Star, HBO, 1998–2004)
The Shield (Shawn Ryan, FX, 2002–2008)
Six Feet Under (Alan Ball, HBO, 2001–2005)
The Sopranos (David Chase, HBO, 1999–2007)
Squid Game (Hwang Dong-hyeok, Netflix, 2021)
Starsky and Hutch (William Blinn, ABC, 1975–1979)
The State (Peter Kosminsky, Channel 4, 2017)
Stranger Things (Duffer Brothers, Netflix, 2016–)
Succession (Jesse Armstrong, HBO, 2018–2023)
Teheran (Moshe Zonder, Dana Eden, Maor Kohn, Apple TV, 2020–2022)
This Is Us (Dan Fogelman, NBC, 2016–2022)
Top of the Lake (Campion & Lee, BBC, 2013)
True Blood (Alan Ball, HBO, 2008–2014)
True Detective (Nic Pizzolato, HBO, 2014–2019)
Twin Peaks (Mark Frost and David Lynch, ABC/Showtime, 1991–199)
Twin Peaks: The Return (or *Twin Peaks* season 3, Mark Frost and David
    Lynch, Showtime, 2017)
Unbelievable (Grant, Waldman, and Chabon, Netflix, 2019)
Vikings (Michael Hirst, 2013–2020, History)
The Walking Dead (Frank Darabont, AMC, 2010–2021)
Weeds (Jenji Kohan, Showtime, 2005–2012)
The West Wing (Aaron Sorkin, NBC, 1999–2006)
When They See Us (Ava DuVernay, Netflix, 2019)
The Wire (David Simon, HBO, 2002–2008)

Index

CPSIA information can be obtained
at www.ICGtesting.com
Printed in the USA
JSHW020005100723
44337JS00001B/1